Songs in The Night

Sandy Cathcart

NEEDLE ROCK
PRESS

Visit Needle Rock Press at www.needlerockpress.com

Visit Sandy Cathcart's Website at www.sandycathcartauthor.com

The above can be found on Facebook.

Songs in The Night

Copyright © 1981 Sandy Cathcart

Second Printing: Copyright © 2016 Sandy Cathcart

Cover photo by Cat Cathcart. Copyright © by Cat Cathcart

Needle Rock Press
341 Flounce Rock Rd.
Prospect, OR 97536

Needle Rock Press books may be purchased in bulk for ministry purposes. For information, please email sandy@sandycathcartauthor.com

ISBN-10: 1943500053
ISBN-13: 978-1943500055 (Needle Rock Press)

first of all
to Christ
for without Him I can do nothing

Then
to my mother
because she "hung in there" in prayer

Where is God my Maker
who gives songs
in the night?

—Job 35:10 (NIV)

About This Book

It is with a singing heart and dancing feet that I come to you today. I first wrote this book over 35 years ago. I typed it on special paper and ran it off on a mimeograph machine. Then my children and I spread the pages all around the living room and collated it by hand. I gathered what little money we had and paid an outside source to staple and trim it. Finally, I gave it away to anyone who wanted it.

Over the years, I 've received letters from people all over the world, as far away as Africa! I've heard from prisoners who saw something among the pages that gave them hope. A young run-a-way wrote about how something she read in *Songs in the Night* made her want to return home and take a chance at forgiveness. I received letters from educators and firemen, young mothers and widows, and an entire lumberjack crew.

What is it among these pages that touches people's hearts?

I suspect it has something to do with the Spirit of God. For whoever seeks shall find, and whoever knocks will discover the door is already open.

Get ready, seeker, the Lover of your soul is out to rescue you!

Contents in Word

Contents in Song

My heart is stirred by a noble theme
as I recite my verses for the king:
my tongue is the pen of a skillful writer.
—Psalm 45:1 (NIV)

I am only a woman,
the same as any other woman,
except for a burning desire to share
what Creator has done in my life.
My husband's name is Cat.
We have five children. At the time of the first printing
they were aged:: Jay (14),
Rob (12), Michelle (9), Clay (6) and Jocelyn (4)

I left a life of hoplessness
for a life of real meaning and purpose.
This is my story
in word and song.

Introduction

Many times while writing this book, I wondered why I was writing it. Seemed like a silly thing to do, since I wasn't famous or had any great words of wisdom to share, yet something compelled me to write. Then one day, when I was discouraged with writing, I sat down to read my Bible.

> Now get up and stand on your feet.
> I have appeared to you to appoint you
> as a servant and as a witness
> of what you have seen of me
> and what I will show you.
> —Acts 26:16 (NIV)

These were words of Jesus to Paul, but they took on new meaning as I realized this was what God had asked me to do in writing this book.

This book is a witness of what I have seen of God and what He has done in my life. My prayer is that your love for God will grow as you read this book and see how He reached out to my family through every circumstance, again and again. I pray your eyes may be opened to see how forgiving and compassionate He has been in your own life.

Truth

ONE THING I APPRECIATE most about God is His trustworthiness. He never lies. He never uses flattery. He never tries to turn things around for his good. He is complete truth. He is faithful. His Word never fails. I can place my hand in His and know He will never let me go.

I spent ten years running away from God just to find He was beside me all the time, careful not to let me go too far, yet willing to let me make my own choice to return to Him.

His love is greater than anything I can understand. If I place my trust in Him, I am freed completely from the chains of fear and worry. He opens doors no human can shut and closes doors no human can open.

He is the same day after day, all-powerful, all-knowing, and always loving toward His children. His justice surpasses men's knowledge, forgiving all who come through His Son, no matter what we've done in the past, or how many times we come with the same thing. He replaces bitterness with compassion, fear with peace, and gives life to those who are dying.

We cannot hide from God. Wherever we go, His light will expose us, yet He gives humans every opportunity to recognize Him as Lord.

There is coming a day when everyone will admit He is Lord with their own tongue. This will not take place through coercion but through absolute and perfect knowledge. Every knee shall bow to Him. That will be a day of celebration for those who follow Christ, but it will be a dreaded day for many others. Many will realize once for all that it was God himself they turned away so many times.

My story is one of surrender. What will be said of your story?

Every Knee Shall Bow
(Based on Romans 14:11)

Every knee shall bow to Him
Every knee shall bow to Him
Of things in heaven and things on earth
Every tongue shall confess He is Lord
Every knee shall bow to Him
Of things on earth and under the earth
Every tongue shall confess He is Lord

Are you ready for the bridegroom
He is coming very soon
Or is your life found wanting
Have you work undone
Are you clothed and waiting in white linen
(chorus)

He is coming with power and great glory
He is coming and every eye shall see
He is coming in the air
We shall rise to meet him there
He is coming soon to take us home
(chorus)

All those who said, "There is no God"
All those who said, "Jesus was only a good man
Not the Son of God"
All those who turned Him away
They won't have one word to say
When they see Him as He is in all His glory
They will bow to the earth and proclaim
"Jesus is Lord."

My friend are you ready for His coming
Or have you put Him off once again
He could come this very day
Then what would you have to say
When every knee shall bow to Him as Lord

Beauty

"WHY DO YOU live the way you do?"

I had been asked the question many times and most often answered with a flippant, meaningless answer that had nothing to do with the real reasons.

"Because it's cheaper," I would say and leave it at that. But, of course, it wasn't the full truth.

Why did I choose to live in a house that could only be reached by driving up a shale rock road that beat both driver and vehicle to pieces? Why did I put up with a half-mile uphill walk from the place where we parked our car to our house in the woods, often having to carry groceries and children? How could I live in a house with no inside walls or ceiling, no plumbing, no electricity, and where every drop of water must be carried? How could I live without the modern conveniences many people take for granted?

Come stand with me, if you will, beneath the majestic cedar, pine and oak trees, and breathe in sweet smelling vanilla and spice. Listen to frog song and chattering squirrels. Look into the clear blue sky and see if you agree this beauty alone is reason enough to leave the busy, polluted city. Rise early with me in the morning, when the sun first rises over the far mountain, and join the chorus of singing birds instead of busy city sounds.

Here in the highlands, time seems to stand still. I can stop and think without interruption. I have time to withdraw from the rest of the world and find out who I really am. To ask myself the questions: "What am I doing here? Where am I going? What is the purpose of my life?"

Seems to me most people don't have the answers to such questions, which may account for all the lies and hypocrisy Cat and I encountered in our young lives; hypocrisy that sent us fleeing from society and escaping to a place deep in the woods.

Here we searched for our dreams and a purpose for living, and here we lived for nearly seven years.

Cat and I experienced many feelings for our mountain home, a combined mixture of love and hate, passionate feelings, leaving indifference to our surroundings an impossibility. Yet, I can honestly say we found the answers we came here to find.

Jesus Set Me Free

Everything I ever wanted
Those things I longed for
Everything I ever needed
I found in His love
All my life-long searching
For a purpose in life
I found in Jesus

(chorus)
He heals the brokenhearted
Sets the captives free
That's me
Yes. That's me
Now my life's spent singing
The song that He gave
Jesus set me free

Free from the world and its ways that enslaved me
Free from the sin and chains that held me
Free from the past and its way that enchained me
Jesus has set me free
(chorus)

Believe

WE ALWAYS TOOK PRIDE in being parents who let our children make their own choices instead of having them believe something only because we believed it. But the day they wanted to go to Sunday School shook us both. To make matters worse, they blurted out their desire in front of our friends who all felt the same way we did about church—that it was a good place to avoid.

The entire group of us had been talking about how our children could make their own choices.

"Is that right?" our oldest son JayJay asked.

"Absolutely," I said.

"Well, we want to go."

Rob and Michelle nodded their heads in agreement. This was not what Cat or I had expected.

"You take them," Cat said to me.

"I'm not about to go to a place full of hypocrites," I said. "They'll just look down on me. You go."

Back and forth we went, while our friends all watched with delight, wondering what church people would do when a family of hippies showed up. And that's exactly what we did.

7

Our family of five dressed in our best clothes, Cat in a sweater and blue jeans and me in a long, homemade dress with a low-cut neck and a ruffled hem. We hiked through the sticky clay mud down the mountain. By the time we reached our vehicle, our feet and the hem of my skirt were a muddy mess, but we all piled in and traveled eighteen miles to Community Bible Church, the only church I knew from my childhood.

The first few Sundays, Cat and I sat in the truck rolling his homemade cigarettes while the kids went to Sunday School. Stores were closed on Sundays in those days, and there were no restaurants in the small town of Central Point, so when the weather grew cold, we ended up inside. The first Sunday wasn't too bad. A few people stared, but we could handle that, and a few others actually greeted us. We especially liked the Praise-the-Lord guy, as we called him. Didn't matter what you said to him, he would always respond with a big smile and say, "Praise the Lord!"

One Sunday, we brought some of our friends to see the Praise-the-Lord guy, and they agreed he was a very strange character.

Russ Rhea was the pastor and also our Sunday School teacher. He was teaching a series of classes on marriage. Some of his ideas about women submitting to their husbands and the two becoming one seemed old-fashioned and prudish. Surely there must be a better way to run a marriage. We were a new generation, promoting free love and no ties. Yet, I remembered the day Cat told me that if he ever caught me in bed with another man, he would shoot to kill both of us. That didn't carry the ring of freedom to me.

Cat and I first met in a tavern. I was the bartender and took his ID to check his age. He was cocky and sure of himself, with seemingly no morals or ties to anyone. I liked his good looks, but I hated the way he was so sure he could get whatever he wanted, whenever he wanted it.

He started coming to the tavern more often, and we began to date. Soon I realized he wasn't at all like most of the guys I knew, guys who just wanted to have a good time and lived only for today, not thinking about what tomorrow might bring. Cat was different, he didn't force himself on me, and he was honest, a characteristic that outshone everything else.

I was still a married woman when Cat met me, but my husband had been living with another woman for some time. Lonely and afraid, I didn't know how long I could keep up the house payments and buy groceries for my three children. I hated work as a bartender, but it was one of the few jobs in our community where I could work nights and be with my children during the day. A neighbor allowed my children to sleep overnight at her house.

I didn't consider myself a drug user, but I did find myself using drugs more often than could be considered social. Drugs helped me get my mind off my fear, but I always ended up having to face my fears in the end. Drugs just prolonged the pain.

One of my friends was a prostitute, and she tried to talk me into going into the same trade. At first, I gave it absolutely no thought, but then, after a hard night's work and turning down dates just to come home to an empty house, her arguments would sound logical. Fear swept over me at the prospect of what I could become.

Cat was the best thing that happened to me during that time. He was kind and, after he moved in with me, he disciplined the children with some very old-fashioned discipline. Seemed strange for a man with his reputation. He had a way with the ladies, and I certainly wasn't the first woman he had lived with.

"Our relationship is different," he said.

I wanted to believe him but was afraid I was just being gullible.

Then, three years later, and after we had been married by a Justice of Peace, we found ourselves sitting in a church of all places, all because our children wanted to attend Sunday School. I attended church when I was young and even accepted Jesus as my Savior. But that was when I was a naïve child. A grown woman should know better. Or should she? Could it be possible the God I believed in as a child, really existed?

Actually, I had always believed in a Supreme Being, but it didn't seem possible we could have a relationship with him. I wasn't sure how to reach him or even if he could be reached. Yet, listening to Pastor Rhea, I began to wonder if Jesus was the way to find a personal relationship with a Living God. Was Jesus the missing part that kept me searching for something even after I had found real love in my husband and family and was living the life of my dreams?

The question stayed with me until one sunny day I looked into a sky completely free of pollution and called out, "God if you're real show me!"

At first I heard nothing over cicada song as I breathed in the aroma of warm oak. Then a whisper spoke in my mind, *Get your Bible.*

I threw up my hands. "I've read the Bible. There isn't anything there to help me."

Get your Bible.

"It's just an old book, full of stories that don't apply anymore." I spoke the words aloud, as if having a conversation with a real person.

Get your Bible.

After the third time, I entered our house and searched for a Bible, finally finding one in our son Rob's trunk. I took it outside, sat in the sun, and began to read. "In the beginning was the Word, and the Word was with God and the Word was God." John 1:1 (NIV)

I stopped and prayed again, "God, if you are real in the person of Jesus Christ, then please let me know." Reading on, I discovered Jesus was the Word and that the Word was Creator. Reading further, I saw the compassion of Jesus for a world of unbelief and cruelty. I read carefully, to see if He was a different kind of person than what he preached.

By the end of the Gospel of John, I knew Jesus was the Christ, the Son of God. And I also knew it would cost me something to follow him.

Throughout the rest of the New Testament, I discovered the disciples who walked with Jesus had believed in him enough to die for their belief, even Jesus' own brother. Somehow the Scriptures opened up to me in a new way. Though I had read them before, this time I had new understanding. Doubt no longer clouded my mind. Jesus *was* who He said He was. He was the Christ, the Son of the Living God, the one and only way to God the Father.

My thoughts turned to Cat. If I chose to follow Jesus, would Cat leave me?

I closed my Bible, unwilling to take that chance.

Questions

Questions deep inside of me
Who am I? What am I meant to be
What am I doin' here? Where am I going
Questions deep inside of me
No one could answer for me
Then I found the answers in Jesus

He can make your life worth living
He can show you what you're meant to be
Deep inside the answer's found
By turnin' your life around
You can have real life in Jesus

Many men today I see trying so hard to be
Working to make a living day by day
The things they work so hard for
Pass away and then they're gone
What's the use of workin' on and on?

I know a place where time just keeps going
Treasures there will never pass away
Treasures there are stored in Him
Who gives our lives real meaning
Store up your treasures in Jesus

If you see the same as me time passes so quickly
Now is the time to start living
Doesn't matter who you are
Where you're at, what you can do
Jesus is waiting for you

He can make your life worth living
He can show you what you're meant to be
Deep inside the answer's found
By turning your life around
You can have real life in Jesus

Decision

FOR MONTHS I BATTLED with my desire to follow Jesus, afraid of what I might have to give up. There were times my entire body trembled to keep from finalizing that decision. Then one Sunday, after hearing the pastor's sermon, I knew I could put it off no longer. With Cat standing to the right of me, the words of truth burned their way into my soul. Jesus was the Way to eternal life, the Key to our existence, the Creator of all things. There was no purpose in life without Him.

When the pastor asked for all eyes to be closed and for those who needed prayer to come forward, I slipped away to the left of Cat, moving from the pew to go pray with Pastor Rhea. I was convinced I was giving up Cat and everything fun in order to do so.

To my surprise, Cat had stepped out of the pew to the right and we met up front. He grabbed my hand and together we learned the first steps on how to start this new life. My first prayer to God was one of thankfulness for His great love, for allowing me to keep my husband, and for not asking me to go through more than I could handle.

Later I discovered Cat had been going through the same battle as me; afraid to tell me for fear he would lose me if he made the decision to follow Christ. It was one of our first lessons in grace. Once we made it our will to do what God wanted us to do, He gave us back the very things we were afraid of losing.

Looking back now, I don't see that I had to give up anything. I can't even remember all the things I was so afraid of giving up. The life I have received is so much more complete than anything I had known before. This new joy isn't one that fades away with the morning light, but is one that stays through the hard times as well as the good. It's an exciting way to live, trusting God for every turn.

As A Little Child
(Based on Mark 11:15)

Would you believe if I told you
Of the love He gave to me
Would you believe if I showed you how He changed me
Would you believe if He stood before you
With arms opened wide
Or would you just say you'd seen an illusion

Come to him in simple faith believing
Open your heart as a little child
And let Him come in
He will open your mind to understanding
If you come to him in simple faith believing

You say you must see a miracle
Before you can believe
Well you are looking at a miracle
Right inside of me
For I was once a slave to this world
Enchained by all its ways
Then Jesus came and gave me life everlasting

For I came to Him in simple faith believing
I opened my heart as a little child
And let Him come in
He opened my mind to understanding
When I came to Him in simple faith believing

Fear

AFTER I MADE A COMMITMENT to follow the way of Jesus, a new fear swept through me. Would Christ accept me? I had deliberately turned away from Him. How complete was God's forgiveness? My mind traveled back over the years and circumstances that led to my turning away from God.

Billy Graham came to Sacramento, California when I was ten years old. After going forward with thousands of other people, I knelt and prayed for God to come into my life. It wasn't till later, as a teenager, that I fully understood that commitment. Then my faith grew until I believed God could and would answer prayer.

As teenagers, a group of us would meet in one of the classrooms before school to pray. We saw prayer after prayer answered, and we believed we could change the world for the better. Then one night, as I was reading my bible alone in my room, something very strange happened.

A voice began to speak.

I couldn't tell whether it was audible or in my mind.

This strange voice said things I had never heard before, turning the entire passage of Scripture around, making it appear as though Satan was good and Jesus was bad. In my mind, I knew such a thing was ridiculous, but this was a real voice and it sounded so convincing.

Looking up, I saw a shadow. But it wasn't on a wall. It was in the center of the room, in mid-air. And it was speaking to me! I was so frightened, I snapped off the light and hid under the covers, hoping the thing would go away.

When I woke the next morning, the shadow and voice were gone, but fear remained. I didn't tell anyone about it, because they would think I was crazy. But I did make a decision that changed the rest of my life. I decided I wouldn't be such a strong Christian. Instead, I would simply slide through life, believing in God, but never saying anything to anyone else. Then, I wouldn't be bothered with these strange shadow creatures in the night.

And it worked.

I never again saw anything remotely close to the shadow voice.

What I didn't realize was that a follower of Christ must be growing at all times. When we aren't growing, our faith begins to die, and that is what happened to me. The doubts the shadow voice had cast upon me that night stayed with me. Instead of dealing with them, I simply tried to push them aside and not think about them.

Slowly, I felt my relationship with God die.

When I was seventeen and attending college, I took a second step away from Christ. It was my first time away from home and I enjoyed dating a lot of guys. Always searching for love, I enjoyed being held and kissed. The guys I dated tried to get me to do more than just kissing and hugging, but I always turned them down, although my hormones begged for more.

One night I was alone in my dorm room thinking about what a good person I had become. Aloud I said, "Well, I'm a pretty good person. I bet I would be just as good if I wasn't a Christian."

A very real voice said, "Oh, you think so?"

Shivers ran across my entire body. I knew without a doubt I was about to find out what kind of person I really was. And that's exactly what happened.

I discovered I was capable of some very bad things. The only thing that had made me different was the power of God's Holy Spirit living in me.

My third and final step away from God came about through a lack of knowledge of the truth of the Scriptures. My desire to be held and hugged led to date rape, and I became pregnant. Instead of turning to God for His advice, I made my own decisions and decided to do things my own way. I just could not trust God to take care of the circumstances once I had messed up everything. So, in order to keep my baby, I married a man I didn't love and who didn't love me.

I stood there in tears on my wedding day, knowing I was turning my back on God. Then my child was born with a serious birth defect. My father told me my son's birth defect was God punishing me for my sin.

I looked at my baby so sweet and innocent in my arms and decided I didn't want anything to do with a God like that.

For the next ten years I walked without God, or so I thought. I made my own decisions and did things my own way, making a big mess of most everything. During that time, I wrote poems of sadness and sorrow, a suicide attempt, divorce and loss.

Now, I was married to a good man who loved me and I had asked God to forgive me for my past wrongs. Could I really expect God to forgive someone like me? Some one who had deliberately turned away from Him?

Who Am I

(Based on Ephesians 1:4)

Who am I Lord that you should choose me
Before the world began you knew me
Who am I Lord that I could choose you
When so many times I refused you
Who am I that you should give your life for me
Open my blinded eyes and let me see
The Lily of the Valley
The Rose of Sharon
The Bright and Morning Star in my life
There to laugh with me
There to cry with me
There to walk each and every mile with me

Given me light for my darkness
Given me strength for my weakness
Given me life in and through me
Jesus in me

The Lily of the Valley
The Rose of Sharon
The Bright and Morning Star in my life
There to laugh with me
There to cry with me
There to walk each and every mile with me

Love

BATTLING MY FEAR of not being accepted by God, brought on a new kind of depression. I felt trapped. There was no life without God, and I wasn't sure I had life with God. If He *had* accepted me, then I must be the least in His kingdom, barely making it through by the skin of my teeth. I was like a dog eating crumbs beneath a fine table. I longed to be loved by God and yearned for intimacy with Him. Was there any hope I would ever see His face?

God knows what we need and when we need it. I had a real need to know His love. So He met that need in a very special way.

Luke 11:9 says, *"Seek and you will find"* (NIV). I sought God with all my heart, yearning to know His love. That is a yearning He will always fulfill.

One day while I was praying, I saw a vision of Jesus on the beach. He walked purposefully toward me, not allowing His eyes to stray from mine. My heart fluttered to think I was actually going to gaze on His face, but as He neared, an overwhelming sense of sorrow filled my soul. How could I have ever turned away from Him? How I wished I could go back and relive my life all over again.

I fell to the ground, not daring to look in His eyes for the pain I feared would be there.

He spoke my name. *"Sandy."*

The sound of His voice speaking my name was like the most beautiful song I had ever heard.

Then He reached down and took my hands in His, guiding me to my feet until I was forced to look into His eyes.

I was terrified of the pain I was sure I would see—pain that I had caused—accusation for my lack of trust. But when I looked, all I saw was love. No trace of sorrow or pain or judgment. Just pure love, like I'd never seen before.

I would have stayed there forever, if it were possible.

The vision of His face never left me, and I now know I am totally forgiven and accepted by God, not because of anything I have done, but because Jesus paid the price for me and I have accepted His payment. When we have done that and really met Him; when we have caught a glimpse of His amazing love for us; then we will gladly take up our cross and follow Him not just in word, but also in every action and deed of our lives.

Wells of Love

Many times I looked at the cross of Jesus
And I'd see His nail-pierced feet
My rising eyes would catch a glimpse
Of nail-scarred hands
Then I'd hang my head in shame
For I could not bear to see His agony
Or look in His eyes for the pain I was sure I'd see
So I'd hang my head in shame
for I could not bear the pain

My life was wrecked with sin and guilt
for the pain He bore
Jesus the perfect Lamb of God
I could not stand the pain I felt inside of me
For I knew it was my sin that caused His pain

Then one day the Savior came to talk with me
I fell at His feet and bowed my head to the ground
He said, "My child, look on my face"
I said, "Lord, I cannot
I love you so, I cannot bear the pain I'll see"
He reached down and lifted me up
I looked in His eyes and to my surprise
I saw no pain . . . I saw no pain . . . I saw no pain
Just wells . . . wells of love
Love He has for me and love He has for you
Love that can't be explained by men's words

Now my life is changed, I have victory
For I am the righteousness of God
My old life is passed away, it's dead and gone
Buried at the cross of Jesus
With Jesus Christ I have risen . . . I've been born again
I looked in His eyes
I saw no pain . . . I saw no pain . . . I saw no pain
Just wells . . . wells of love
Love He has for me and love He has for you
Love that can't be explained by men's words

Music

SEEMED LIKE EVERYONE on the mountain played guitar. Long winter nights without television needed to be filled with some kind of entertainment, so Cat and I decided to learn how to play.

We visited a music store and bought a book. We already had an old clunker of a guitar. It should do. We practiced and studied with the hopes of making beautiful music. By the time we got to "Twinkle, Twinkle, Little Star," I was discouraged and Cat quit.

This wasn't the kind of beautiful music we had in mind.

Darrell, an ex-school teacher who lived on the mountain, informed us the best way to learn was from other guitar players. He began bringing his guitar with him and would play a song about rolling in your sweet baby's arms and another simple rhythm while I struggled to keep up. His patience was incredible. He would play and play while I plunked along saying, "One more time, Darrell, I just about have it."

One day, I played right along with Darrell without skipping a beat. What a thrill! But that was just a taste of sweeter things to come. Playing one song gets old fast. I would try playing familiar songs from a music book, but failed every time.

Alone, during one of my practice sessions, I thought I would just try playing and singing something . . . anything . . . perhaps it might resemble a song. After all, there are many different kinds of music in the world.

To my surprise, what came out actually sounded like a song. The words even had a message. Seemed like I could express my feelings through music better than by mere conversation.

Soon, I was singing my prayers to God. Often my songs would start with questions but end with answers. God was using music as a way of communicating with me. I never dreamed such a thing could happen. There were times a song would just pop out of nowhere, the whole thing, all at once. Those were special songs, because I was convinced they came to me completely through the power of God.

Being able to express myself through music had been one of my lifelong desires. Now, it seemed as if God had just bundled it up as a gift and handed it to me. That's when I realized the meaning of Matthew 7:11 (NIV).

> "If you then, though you are evil,
> know how to give good gifts to your children,
> how much more will your Father in heaven
> give good gifts to those who ask Him!"

If God was giving me a gift of music, how could I not give it back to Him as a gift of service?

I Can't Believe
(Based on Ephesians 1:4-8)

Some people think
They have something to offer God
Others think they have nothing at all
God isn't interested in what we have to offer Him
It's our love, our self, that God wants most of all

He's the same God today as yesterday
His pleasure is in knowing that we love Him
I can't believe. No. It really is astounding
What Jesus Christ, Himself, has done in me

I can't believe
What He has done in me
I can't believe. No. It really is astounding.
The God over all the universe
Reached down in love to one such as me

He took my broken life
Emptied me of self
Then He filled me with His Holy Spirit
I can't believe. No. It really is astounding
What Jesus Christ, Himself, has done in me
The God over all the universe
Reached down in love to one such as me

Gifts

CHRISTMAS WAS NEARING. Snow covered the ground, and we hadn't been off the mountain in a couple of weeks because fuel was a luxury. Cat and I were both out of work, as were most of our neighbors, and we all needed to conserve money any way we could. We had little food and no money for gifts, but this Christmas was our first to celebrate the birth of Jesus Christ and the life He had given us together. Everything took on new meaning as we realized the love of God was the greatest gift of all.

We had just completed decorating our tree with pinecones and popcorn strings when we heard voices outside. Soon the dogs were barking. Anyone coming to our house would have to traipse through the mud and snow a half-mile up hill. Peering through the window, I couldn't believe my eyes.

"It's Marvin," I said, "the Praise-the-Lord guy and his family. How did they ever find us?"

Cat pulled on his boots and went to meet them. Soon children's laughter filled the house along with excited confusion of boots being pulled on and off. The children all made their exit to play in the snow while the adults hovered around the wood heater.

These were our first visitors from the church. They had hiked up the mountain with a tiny baby and two older boys. We enjoyed a fun afternoon of sharing our lives together. Then, before leaving, Marvin turned to us. "Will you accept some groceries as a gift?"

Thinking he must have brought a basket of food as some people do for Christmas, Cat said, "Sure."

Cat and the boys hiked back down to the car with Marvin to retrieve the groceries. Not just a basket of food, but several bags! A whole crate of oranges, which was our favorite. There were gifts of socks and toilet paper, canned vegetables and a frozen turkey. Some of our neighbors helped carry the gifts to our house. We were astounded, as were our neighbors.

"Why are you so generous?" I asked.

Marvin flashed his enormous smile and said, "Praise the Lord! We wanted to do this as brothers and sisters in the Lord. The Lord has blessed us, so we want to bless you. We don't expect a thing in return."

After they left, we celebrated by going through all the bags to see what delectable things our friends had brought. Soon there was more knocking on our door. Cat opened it to find all of our neighbors crowded together to see what had happened and why. It was a special time to be able to share some of the gifts of food and the gift of real love that asks for nothing in return.

It was remarkable Marvin had found our house in the first place. With no directions other than the fact you can see Chimney Rock from our house, he had traveled over eighteen miles and found us. Other potential visitors with more exact directions had become lost and given up before finding our place.

This was a real lesson to us in the power and love of God. Some of the hardness in our hearts began to melt away, birthing a new ability to trust. Through our friends' generosity, we had experienced love. Love that goes that extra mile, giving without expecting anything in return. Love that knows no barriers or bounds, but just keeps on truckin'! Love that can only come from God living within us.

Later, when we knew Marvin better and no longer called him the Praise-the-Lord guy, he shared what the Lord had done for him through that experience.

Cat and I tended to carry prejudice for people we termed as "rednecks," which is how we saw Marvin. He had prejudice for people he termed as "hippies," which is how he saw us. Over the months of sharing our lives together in many ways, the prejudices on both sides melted away, and all of us realized we were a part of the family of God, each and every one of us.

Love From The Father

Love . . . everyone really wants love
No one . . . really wants to do without love
They search and they seek
And they look everywhere to find it
They devote their whole lives
And give everthing to get it
Because we who believe
Hold back on God's love
They don't see it

(chorus)
Love from the Father through the Son to us
Love when He gave His only Son
Love from the Father should flow in and through us
Love should reach out to everyone

Have you been trying to live this life your way
Why not try and live this life God's way
Give your whole life to Him
And He will come in and live through you
Whether great or small give to Him all your troubles
Have you forsaken or have you forgotten
Your first love
(chorus)

Love . . . from the Father inside us
Like a river should flow in and through us
Then the whole world will see
And really believe God is love
Those who are seeking
With open hearts will start reaching for our love
Those who are lost
Will learn Christ paid the cost
For He is love

Unbelief

I REMEMBER SOME GOOD TIMES on the mountain; times when we would get together and share a meal and lively conversation. It was a matter of preservation as well as fellowship, because it was easier to cook one meal for all of us than it was for each of us to cook our own. So we met at Jeanie's, because she had the biggest house. During those times, someone would always bring up religion in some way. Often, we were asked what we thought of the Bible.

On this day, we all huddled around the wood heater with steaming bowls of chicken and dumplings. The air was filled with contradicting smells of delicious food and unwashed bodies.

"Do you think the Bible has the answers?" Darrell asked.

"Don't know yet," Cat said around a mouthful of dumpling. "But we'll let you know when we find out."

A few months later, I believed I knew the answer. Jesus was who He said He was, Creator, the Son of the Living God. He had the power to change people's lives and set them free from bondage to the things that put chains around us. Cat and I had both experienced that life-changing power. Jesus gave real meaning to life and filled the empty spot that never seemed to go away. I thought everyone would want to know.

To my surprise, my friends didn't want to hear one word. Darrell had asked questions more than anyone. I was sure he would want to know about this awesome freedom.

"We found the answers we were looking for," I told Darrell one day. "Not in religion, or even in the church, but in the person of Jesus."

Darrell picked up his guitar, gave me a half smile and said, "That's nice." Then he walked out of our house and stayed away. I never even got a chance to tell him what Jesus meant to me.

Next, I sent a letter to Cat's Mom and Dad, telling them of our changed lives. Cat had been estranged from his family for nearly a decade, but one of the first things he did as a new believer was open the door of communication. His parents had sent him to church as a boy and he thought they would be excited about his belief in Jesus. But they never once mentioned it in their letters.

Finally, we found the opportunity to travel over six hundred miles to see them. It was an uneasy reunion. A lot of changes happened in eight years of separation. The first time we sat down to enjoy a meal together Cat's Mom said, "We don't want to hear anything about your religious beliefs. We're glad you found something good for you, but we don't need it."

Obviously they thought we would preach at them, and they were probably right. In our exuberance we ended up chasing all our friends and family away, but Cat wanted so badly to share his faith with his family. A faith that completely changed his life, taking away bitterness that had separated him from his parents for so long. A faith in a God that reaches out to people of every country and culture in the world, breaking all barriers, whether of time or race. We sat there pushing food around on our plates, brokenhearted that we were unable to share the most important thing that had ever happened to us.

We had good news and had found the answers to the most important questions of life, but none of our friends and family wanted to know. Just days earlier, people had asked us some of the same questions for which we now had answers.

I was amazed when I later found these words in Matthew 13:15 (NIV). *"For this people's heart has become calloused; they hardly hear with their ears, and they have closed their eyes, Otherwise they might see with their eyes, hear with their ears, understand with their hearts and turn, and I would heal them."*

Cat and I had once been those people with closed eyes and closed ears, but finally our ears and eyes were opened, and we found healing.

Yes. Jesus is real, but we also have a very real enemy who takes pleasure in closing people's eyes to the truth. It's easy for our enemy to blind us when the exuberance of new Christians outweighs our knowledge and wisdom.

Cat would eventually learn that love is the most important thing; not just showing love, but truly loving others. Amazing that God gave us the ability to do just that through the power of His Holy Spirit. We would also learn that we can pray for others, that God will not give them over to an unbelieving spirit; that He will heal them in the same way He healed us.

Yes. I've seen people with cold hearts and closed minds, but I've also seen some of those same people light up like the sun when blindness has been lifted from their eyes and they see the truth for the first time. I will keep on singing my songs and telling others of Jesus for as long as I live on this earth. I want to tell the whole world Jesus love them, because He really does!

I Want to Tell The World

(Based on Matthew 24; John 1:1-14 & 3:16-19
& Revelation 6:12-17
Chorus based on Matthew 13:14-15)

The streets are filled with people
Rushing to and fro
Everyone is so busy
They've all got somewhere to go
No one seems to know the reason
Why they're going
Tomorrow the purpose of their ventures
Will be forgotten
Man's efforts never pass
The test of time
He's here and gone and no one knows
He's even been
I can hear the people
And they're crying
And I know that they
Are just dying
They don't know why they were born
Or where they're going
They always are too busy
To even listen

(Chorus)
I want to tell the world
"Jesus loves you"
Yes, I want to tell the whole world
"Jesus loves you"
But they've got their fingers in their ears
And their backs turned to me
How can you show them how to see
When their eyes are closed

Jesus came to this earth
In peace and love
God sent Him down to us
Right from heaven above
He brought to us a real reason
For living in a world of confusion
But men loved darkness more than the light
That shone through Him
They crucified the Son of God
And buried Him
But He arose from death in victory
He is alive to bring new life today
(Chorus)

The streets are now all empty
The people are all gone
The sun and moon turned black
The stars are fallen
Everyone's gone to the hills
To find a hiding place
Many cry out for death
Fear is on every face
They cry out to God
"You never showed me"
When all the time their eyes were closed
So they couldn't see
The truth that was taught
Throughout history
Of the one way that they could be set free
Through Jesus Christ the Son of God
Through Jesus Christ the Son of God
(Chorus)

Loneliness

THREE MONTHS PASSED, and I couldn't get off the mountain. Our vehicle had broken down, and we had no phone, so the only people I communicated with were my husband and children. Cat hiked out each day to ride with a neighbor to work, but I was completely cut off from society. I wondered why no one from church seemed to miss us. I had no way of letting them know of our predicament, but surely someone would care enough to reach out.

My thoughts traveled to the people we had met at church. Many had reached out to us, and I thought they really cared, but now I was beginning to wonder. I understood the logistical challenge of us living a long way from town, but surely they could make one visit.

As the days passed, my heart began to grow bitter. It seemed as if no one truly cared about us. Finally, I told God how I felt.

"Doesn't anyone care?" I asked.

Softly, He spoke to my heart, letting me know people did care, but they were busy with their own lives and not aware we had a need. If they had known we were stranded, they would have found some way to help us, or at least come for a visit.

Finally, the day came when our car was fixed. I had a doctor's appointment, among many other chores, while in town. While I sat in the waiting room, a woman from church entered.

"How are you?" I asked as she sat across from me. Her fingers clutched her purse and her eyes never quite met mine.

"I've seen better days," she admitted. "I've been going through depression. I'm here to see a counselor."

I couldn't believe my ears. Her makeup was perfect and her clothing stylish. She was a beautiful woman with lovely skin and a trim figure. Her life seemed so perfect. How could she be lonely or depressed?

I had never been to her house, though I thought about doing so several times. Thinking she was too busy for company, I always talked myself out of it. Now here she was, turning to a doctor for help when her Christian brothers and sisters could have come alongside her. I was her Christian sister, what had I done to help meet her need?

Realization hit me hard. I was guilty of the very thing I had been feeling so self-righteous about others not doing for me. Unable to hold back tears on the way home, I kept asking myself how I could have been so blind. Was it because I had been so busy feeling sorry for myself I failed to see others had needs? It's easy to point the finger at others and not see we are doing the very same thing, maybe in different ways, but with the same result of hurting someone.

"Lord," I prayed, "help me to love others the way you love, forgetting about myself and seeing their need."

Step on Your Neighbor

(Based on Matthew 5:42-48 and 18:21-35)

Many of us who call ourselves Christians
Really put a shame to that claim
For if we really are of Jesus
We would be more Christ-like in His name
Our feelings get hurt far too easily
Oh how many times I've felt that myself
But when our feelings are hurt
It's that much harder
To love the one who's done the hurt

(chorus)
Step on your neighbor yeah
Step on your neighbor ah
He doesn't matter that much
Step on your neighbor yeah
Step on your neighbor
After all he's done it to you
Step on your neighbor yeah
Step on your neighbor
Seems to be the thing to do
Step on your neighbor yeah
Step on your neighbor
Before he steps on you

I've heard the question asked
"Why should I do anything for them
They've never done anything for me"
I've seen hate returned for hate
Our pride tells us we've been treated unfairly
When Jesus says to turn the other cheek
Often when someone falls by the wayside
We pass by without even one glance

37

We're too busy worrying about our own lives
To care about what's happening to someone else
(chorus)

Jesus said to give without expecting
Anything at all in return
Yeah we are to love and keep right on loving
Though the more we love the less we are loved
Jesus said to forgive one another
Seventy times seven for the same thing
Yeah we are to forgive when they
Don't even ask forgiveness
Forgive them in Jesus' name

Love one another yeah
Love one another
That's what Jesus said
Love your neighbor as yourself
Everyone is the same
Love your enemies. Pray for them
Bless those that persecute you
Love one another and then when you fail
Let Jesus love through you
Let Jesus love through you

Work

CAT HAD BEEN OUT OF A REGULAR JOB for several months. Because of a crippling disease called rheumatoid arthritis, most employers would turn him away once they saw his medical record. Now, as a Christian, he believed he should be working to make a living for his family. So, we began to pray for the Lord to give Cat a job.

As we prayed, my mind went back to a time when Cat had a job falling trees. He would rise before dawn and take our old Dodge flatbed truck to a place nearly sixty miles away. He wouldn't return until the sun had already set. The hillside was so steep he would often hold the chainsaw with one hand while steadying himself with the other. He and Ron faced danger every day.

Cat didn't mind the hard work or the danger, but the arthritis racked his body with pain. His shoulders and arms would ache to the point he couldn't use them. One time, he spent three nights in a row walking back and forth under the night sky, unable to sleep because of pain. Then he would pour himself back into the truck as soon as the sun began to rise and head off to work once again.

I worried about Cat using a chainsaw on that steep hillside with so little sleep. I kept thinking about my friend from high school whose father had died when a falling tree bucked up and hit him in the chest.

We were both thankful when a job offer came for Cat to work as a warehouseman for a valley grocery store. He would have to cut his hair and shave his beard, but it was a regular job, something we had long prayed for.

But the question plagued us—could Cat hold the job long term? What if swelling and pain from arthritis caused him to miss work? His new employer wouldn't keep him long in that case.

Convinced it was God's will for him to work, Cat decided to trust God to take care of the pain problem. He believed if he did what God wanted him to do, then God would give him the strength to do it.

First the beard came off. We had traveled to my parent's house so Cat could shave. All the way home the kids and I stared at him. He looked like a completely different man. I tried to memorize every crevice of his newly shaved face for fear I wouldn't recognize my own husband if I saw him from a distance.

Cat soon tired of our staring. "Why don't you guys find something else to stare at?" he said.

Next, the hair was cut. Now, he looked altogether different, and I was utterly convinced I wouldn't recognize him in a crowd. The kids and I couldn't resist teasing him. He always took it well, but I would catcAh a glimpse of something in his eyes and often wondered what he was thinking.

People made comments about Cat's new appearance. Old friends would tease him about going "straight." Our new friends would praise him for "cleaning up his act." A lot of people thought Christians should look a certain way. A lot of our old friends backed off, thinking they would have to shave and cut their hair to become a Christian. They didn't realize God accepts us just the way we are and cleans us up on the inside.

It bothered Cat that people looked at him differently since he cut his hair and shaved his beard. He was still the same person and worked just as hard as before. His appearance was the only thing that had changed. Yet people treated him as if he had become a different kind of person.

"Can't they see I changed long before I cut my hair?" He asked.

His question made me look at things differently. How many times had I taken people for face value, never looking past their appearance. "Lord," I prayed, please help me see others the way you see them."

I was amazed when I found these words in Matthew 9:36-37 (NIV). *"Jesus went through all the towns and villages, teaching in their synagogues, preaching the good news of the Kingdom and healing every disease and sickness. When He saw the crowds, He had compassion on them, because they were harassed and helpless, like sheep without a shepherd."*

How often had I felt harassed and helpless?

Jesus saw everyone that way—people of high standing and people of low standing, rich or poor. He saw them all as helpless, and He had compassion on each and every one. I decided that is how we should see others, in their need for the life only Jesus can give. Surely, we shouldn't require a person to change on the outside before we can have compassion on them.

This new knowledge began a ritual for me of asking God to help me see the heart of people and not merely look on the outside. I discovered brokenness where I once saw haughtiness; humility where I once saw pride; and fear where I once saw anger. I not only made new friends, but even enemies became friends, and I saw myself in a different way as well . . . as one in need of grace and as one who is a part of the family of Christ

Christ is All
(Based on Colossians 3)

(chorus)
Christ is all
And in all
Who have received Him
Into their life
Christ is all
And in all
Give Him glory
Alleluia

Shout it from the mountaintop
It matters not what color you are
Neither Greek nor Jew
Nor rich nor poor
Put on the whole creation of Christ
Old things are passed away
All is become new
(chorus)

If you have accepted Him
Then you are dead and your life is hid
With Christ in God
When Christ who is our life
Shall appear
Then shall we also
Appear with Him in glory
(chorus)

Healing

CAT ACCEPTED THE JOB as warehouseman. As the weeks passed, I wondered how long it would be before arthritis would keep him from work. He believed the Lord had healed him. I hoped He had, but was fearful He had not. Doctors had little hope Cat would ever improve. They only hoped to contain the arthritis before it spread throughout his entire body, leaving him crippled for life.

Whenever I saw Cat hold his arm in pain, I was sure he was in trouble. Later, he shared he did have pain at times, but he would always give it to the Lord right away, claiming the promises out of the Word. Then the day finally came when he no longer felt pain. We rejoiced both for the healing and for the fact he could hold his job long term.

When Cat realized the pain was gone, he began to tell other people how they could be healed. He was suddenly convinced that no Christian ever had to be sick. It took a serious bout of flu to convince him the Lord doesn't heal everyone every time. Then he accepted God's gift of healing with praise, realizing it was God's grace that met him in our hour of need. It wasn't for us to question why God meets certain needs and not others.

Three years later, Cat returned to the doctor for an x-ray of his back. The doctor was amazed at what he saw and just kept shaking his head. Straight bones showed absolutely no sign of arthritis.

We thanked God for the visible proof of what Cat had already accepted by faith.

Looking back, it is good to see God is in control. He sees the future, while we are limited to the present and past. As we apply God's Word to our lives, we build up our faith and trust as we see Him use every circumstance for our good. Then, when the time comes when we can't see any possible good in a situation, we can find peace in the fact we know God is in control, because He has shown us His power time after time. His faithfulness is beyond human understanding.

How Can I Say Thank You Lord

(Based on Numbers 11)

How can I say thank you Lord
For the wonders you've done in my life
There are no words to express
All the love that I feel inside

Thank you Lord, praise your name
Thank you Lord, for staying the same
Thank you Lord, praise your name
The God of Israel is still the same

When the children of Israel were thirsty
You gave them sweet water to drink
When they were hungry
You gave them manna
And still they complained
So often Lord, I do the same
And wonder why you don't give up on me
Yet you're always there
Reaching out your hand
To pick me up and bring me back once again

Thank you Lord, praise your name
Thank you Lord, for staying the same
Thank you Lord, praise your name
The God of Israel is still the same

Sunrise

IT WAS A BEAUTIFUL MORNING. The sun had just risen above the afar ridge, bathing the mountainside in sunlight. With no inside walls or insulation, we shivered in our beds, but the sunlight pierced through the cold, bringing warmth to our chilled bodies. Warm sunshine and clear skies were always special following a cold, moonless night.

On such mornings, I would rise and take my guitar to a place in the sunshine and praise God in song among all that untouched beauty. Warmth would reach down to my inner being, making me glad to be alive.

That's the way it was in my life—the darker the storm, the harder the troubles, the deeper the appreciation of the peaceful, non-eventful days. We could always look forward to a sunrise even after the darkest night.

This morning was extra special, because I had just completed the words of a song that expressed the way I felt about the sunrise. Even though I had never sung a solo in my life, I knew the Lord was asking me to share this song with others. I knew it, because He had touched my heart through the Scriptures, letting me know when He gives a gift to one of His children, He expects that child to share it with others.

I could only play a few chords on the guitar and wasn't sure if I had a singing voice, but I knew there was a real message in the songs the Lord had given me. Many times the songs had ministered to my own needs.

"Okay," I told the Lord, "I'll do it." First I tried getting other singers to share my songs, but they all turned me down, so I asked God to give me strength and courage to do it myself. "And," I said, "You'll have to give me a voice, because the message will be lost if I sound terrible."

The night arrived when I was to sing in front of my entire church congregation. I don't remember ever being as frightened as I was that night. My hands shook, my heart beat out a staccato rhythm, and I felt faint. I thought about leaving through the back door as doubts began to plague me. Maybe my songs weren't really songs at all. My hands were shaking so badly I feared I couldn't play the guitar.

Please Lord, I prayed. *Will you take control of me and sing through me. Will you please fill me with your peace that passes all understanding.*

Nothing seemed to happen. If anything, I was shaking all the more.

Then the pastor called my name to come up and sing. I opened my mouth to tell him I couldn't do it, but no words came out. So, I picked up my guitar and walked to the front of the church, climbing the steps to the stage and praying for peace all the way, but never feeling a sense of peace. I kept my eyes down, afraid to look at the people. Then a strange thing happened.

As I turned to face the congregation, peace filled my soul.

I had it in my mind to sing quietly in case my voice wasn't very good, but instead a strong, beautiful voice came through the microphone. I sang, knowing it was not just me singing the song, but the Holy Spirit in me, taking His message to His people who were in need.

I'll never forget that night and how the Holy Spirit took control, but the thing I remember most is the lesson learned. God does keep His promises. He does exactly what He says He will. At the same time, He expects us to take that first step of trust.

He didn't give me the peace I longed for until I took that step of trust by getting up to sing the song. Then peace was there when I needed it most.

Since then, I have sung many times in many different places, always nervous and afraid beforehand, but the Lord always gives me peace that passes all understanding *after* I have taken that step of trust in doing what He has given me to do.

After the Storm has Passed
(Based on Psalm 30:5)

When I arise in the morning time
And see the sun has risen
I feel the warmth of sunshine
Flowing through my whole being
This is the dawning of a new day
I feel renewed
My tired body has had its rest; my spirit is revived
Lord, I thank you for this day
Live your wondrous life through me
Fill me with your Holy Spirit
Let your light so shine through me

(chorus)
How wondrous is the love that Christ has given to me
How beautiful each day He gives new life to me
And the peace that passes understanding
He gave to me and still
I feel that blessed peace inside
Whenever the storm clouds roll
Joy comes in the morning
After the storm has passed
And the light of the sun shines
Through the parted clouds

When He arose a new morning came
For all those who believe His name
He is the only begotten of God
Jesus Christ, the Son of God
He's called the Bright and Morning Star
The Light of the World
Jesus Christ, the same yesterday, today and forever
When I gave my life to Him
He filled me with Himself
God's Holy Spirit filled my soul
Now I am completely whole
(chorus)

Broken

SEEMED LIKE EVERYTHING WAS FALLING APART. We tried so hard to raise animals and make a living off our land, and time and time again something would get into our garden just before harvest and destroy it. Our vehicle was always breaking down, because of the shale rock road leading to our place. Our house was always in an unfinished state, because of a lack of money. And now it seemed as if we were losing all our animals.

Our milk goat died of pneumonia. A tree fell on our billy goat and broke his neck. We had to give away our favorite dog, because he was chasing chickens. And our milk cow and the little beef cow we were raising were lost in someone else's cattle drive.

We were tired. Tired of fixing fences just to have them broken in another spot an hour later. Tired of carrying water and chasing cows. Tired of heating and reheating dishwater and always having to keep a fire going. Tired of being cold all winter long and working so hard simply to survive.

It was with these thoughts I awoke this morning, along with the disappointment of all our unrealized dreams for this, our home in the country. Why didn't God do something to change our circumstances?

Rising before the sun, I started a fire and cooked breakfast for Cat, sending him off to work. Then I prepared breakfast for our children, sending Jay, Rob and Michelle down to the bus stop. Next, I stoked the fire and carried two five-gallon buckets down to the stream, filled them with water, and hauled them back up the hill. Then I poured the water into big pans to heat for dishwater.

Having finished the rest of the household chores. I put Jocelyn down for a nap and bundled Clay to go out with me to feed the animals. We broke the ice off the water troughs and fed the chickens, rabbits and cow. Then we headed for the pigpen.

The pig was out!

He had broken the wire and busted right through the middle.

Clay went off to play while I went after the pig.

I found the pig at the bottom of our property, and it took me over an hour to chase him back up the hill and into his pen. Then I retrieved a hammer and a bag of nails and fixed the pen. When I finished and took a step away, the pig burst through again, this time grunting and snorting like a wild boar.

I went after him again, but it took me longer to herd him back into his pen. I found some boards and nailed them to posts, but even while I was nailing them he was trying to get out. Finally he burst through, sending the boards and me flying through the air.

I fell on some rocks, putting a big gash in my arm.

"That's it Lord!" I hollered. "That's your pig. You can do whatever you want with him."

Stomping back up to the house, I thought of Cat who had worked so hard. Now, after coming home from work exhausted, he would have to chase the pig and fix the pen. Seemed like I always had bad news for him lately. How my heart ached for him.

Looking up through the pine and fir trees and into a clear country sky I said, "Lord, don't you even care?"

Standing there, I heard a whisper of a voice. *"Of course I do."*

That's all it took. That gentle voice sent assurance into my heart that something bigger was at work here.

When Cat returned home, I shared my experience with him. Together, realizing God did care, we took a new look at why He was allowing these things to happen. Before, we just thought these events were attacks from the enemy of our souls, so we fought against them. Now, we saw it might actually be God we were fighting. That was certainly a war we would never win.

That night, as our little family sat over a meal of wild venison and potatoes, Cat prayed, "Lord, if any more animals die in the next week, we will take that as a sign from you that you do not want us to raise animals."

The very next day, Cat found two dead rabbits in the pen. We had never lost a rabbit before, so we took it as a direct answer from God. The animals had to go. We sold the rest of the rabbits, our milk cow, and all but a few chickens. Next we had the pig butchered. That was the best meat we ever ate! Without the hassle of raising animals, we now had time to enjoy our country home and realize some of our dreams. We also had more time to reach out and share God's love with others.

Now, when troubles come our way, instead of feeling persecuted and getting depressed or mad, we endeavor to remind each other that God really does care about our family, and He has a purpose in each and every thing that happens to us. We are able to look beyond our troubles with joy to see what new exciting thing God is doing in our lives.

What a wonderful God we serve!

The big thing is not to ask, "Why?" but to have trust that God is using every circumstance to bring about His perfect plan for our lives, even though we can't see what good could possibly come out of it. He has promised His strength to see us through. It only takes a little faith to believe God wants only the best for His children.

Is My Will Broken
(Based on Hebrews 4:12)

Is my will broken
Is your light shining through
Is my will broken
Will I do what you'd have me to do
Is my will broken
Is your light shining through
How long, Lord, till I learn to wait on you

(Chorus)
Not my will but Thine be done
My spirit and soul united as one
As your Living Word, sharper than any two-edge sword
Piercing the innermost part of me, setting my spirit free
Let your light shine through
Till all the darkened world May see you

What about the confusion inside of me
What about that stubborn part of me
What about my foolish vanity
What about my curiosity
When will your light expose me
open my eyes and let me see
When trials seem to surround me
let me not question why
because they are from you, Lord
make me willing to accept

Is my pride forsaken
Is your love flowing through
Is my self forgotten
Will I do what you'd have me to do
Is my will broken
Is your light shining through
How long, Lord, till I learn to wait on you

Hitchhiker

I WAS RUNNING LATE. JayJay had a dentist appointment, and I had to pick him up at school. I bundled Clay and Jocelyn into the backseat of the Jeepster and headed down the road. I was driving faster than usual, thinking of how important this appointment was to my son.

JayJay had been born with a cleft palate and lip, and he had already undergone several corrective surgeries. Today's appointment of putting braces on his teeth was to be the final step of correction. I was proud of the way he had never complained or felt sorry for himself. I didn't want to be late for this appointment.

The shocks on our Jeepster were so bad that every time I turned a corner, it would sway all over the place. I had just rounded a corner and was trying to straighten the Jeepster when Clay hollered from the backseat.

"Mom! Look out!"

A man was standing in the middle of the gravel road.

I stomped on the brakes.

The man barely stepped out of the way before the Jeepster slid to a stop. He was smiling at me as if he knew me. I wasn't sure, but he looked a little like our friend, Mad Dog.

Mad Dog was a local character who didn't own a car. All of us who lived on the mountain would give him a ride whenever we saw him. He was always polite, though not too clean. But this man was not Mad Dog. I could tell because he had already opened the door and jumped in. I had never seen this guy before!

"My husband doesn't allow me to pick up hitchhikers," I said. "I thought you were Mad Dog."

"A lot of people make that mistake," he said. "Mad Dog's out of town. I'm Kenny."

"Mom," Clay squealed. "You're not supposed to pick up hitchhikers."

"My son's right, I said. "We don't pick up hitchhikers."

Making no move to get out of the car, Kenny turned to Clay, "I'm not really a hitchhiker, son, since I'm a friend of your mother's friend."

Clay sniffled, tears forming in his eyes. "Dad's not going to like this."

Something seemed really wrong with the way Kenny was acting, but we were a long way from any neighbors, and I didn't see how I could make him leave, short of pushing him out the door. He was a lot bigger than me and probably a lot stronger.

I put the Jeepster in gear and started back down the road.

"Where are you headed?" Kenny asked.

"White City."

"Great! That's where I'm headed."

Kenny had rattled me so much that I had forgotten I had to drive the opposite direction to pick up JayJay. I took my foot off the gas pedal. "I'm sorry," I said. "I have to pick up my son in Eagle Point. You should probably get a ride with someone else."

Kenny flashed a big smile. "Eagle Point is even better."

Seemed like a strange answer. If White City was perfect, how could the opposite direction be even better? I put my foot back on the gas pedal feeling more nervous with each passing minute.

"So, how does this thing handle off road," Kenny asked.

"Great. That's why we bought it."

"What kind of gas mileage does it get?"

"Not good."

"Looks like you need to get gas soon."

"Yep."

"Seems to handle pretty good on gravel."

"It's okay," I said, "but you have to stay on top of it."

"How's that?"

"It's a fight going down the road."

"Doesn't seem that bad to me."

Tiring of his many questions, I said, "Hang on." I accellerated and rounded the next corner, causing the Jeepster to sway crazily back and forth.

"Whee!" Clay said in the back seat. He knew I had the car under control, but Kenny did not. He shot bolt upright, clinging to the door on one side and the dashboard on the other.

For the next five minutes, Kenny remained quiet, but as we neared Mad Dog's house his hands began to shake. He pulled out a pack of cigarettes. "Have any matches?" he asked.

"No," I said. "Cat gave up smoking quite a while ago."

Ignoring my answer, he searched through the glove compartment and under the seat. Then he checked between the seats. I figured he was probably in need of drugs and hadn't been able to get any for a while. Otherwise, why was he shaking so badly?

A strange thing happened when we reached paved road. I had already noticed there were no other vehicles either coming or going and, though it was a warm spring day, not one person was outside. Usually people were out checking on their animals or taking care of outside chores. When we neared the next corner, a man came running out of his house pointing at us. I didn't know the man, and I didn't see any reason why we should grab his attention.

Meanwhile, Kenny was talking about his life on the mountain. Several people we knew came up in his story—people Cat and I had called friends before we made the choice to follow Christ—people who no longer wanted to have anything to do with us. The drug scene was heavy, and I felt sorry that people were trapped in their addictions. I also felt sorry for Kenny as his agitation grew to panic state. At the same time, I was beginning to feel more than a little nervous about having him in the car with my children. Was he a dangerous man?

Finally, we crossed Highway 140 and headed down the last stretch of country roads before entering the outskirts of Eagle Point. Still, there were no other cars traveling the road and no people outside, other than the man who pointed at us.

"Where are we?" Kenny asked.

I glanced at him to see if he was kidding. If he lived here, then he certainly should know where we were, since Eagle Point was the closest town in the vicinity. It was just over the next hill, and I was very glad. Shivers of fear crawled up and down my legs. Recently, a friend of ours had been shot and killed in a drug war, and several other shootings had taken place in the span of a few weeks. Cat had wanted me to purchase a gun and learn how to use it.

"Carry it in the car for protection," Cat had said.

Part of me wished I had taken Cat's advice, but another part was glad I hadn't. Dad had always told me never to point a gun at anyone unless I intended to kill them, and I didn't think I could ever actually pull the trigger on a killing shot. And what if a gun had been between the seats when Kenny was searching for matches? Would he have used it on my children and me? What did I really know about this man?

At last, we rounded the last hill coming into view of the city. A few houses lined the right side of the road while open fields stretched across the left. As we neared an intersection where Riley Road connected from the left, a big white car backed out of a driveway to my right. I slowed to a stop in order to allow the driver to move out of the way, but instead, he stopped, with his car blocking both lanes.

To my astonishment, the driver opened the door and stood, leaning his arms across the top of the car. He pointed a gun straight at our faces!

"Mommy!" Clay burst into tears.

Jocelyn, who had been sleeping in the seat beside him, joined his sobs. I kept my eyes peeled on the man with the gun, my right hand on the gearshift, and my left on the steering wheel, wondering if I should try to make a run for it. The car in front of us was unmarked, and the man with the gun wore no uniform, but something about him made me think he might be a cop, which is what we called policemen in those days.

I turned to Kenny, "Are you wanted?"

His body was rigid with fear. His eyes were wide and his mouth open. His breathing was rapid and erratic. I doubted if he even heard my question. Then I realized his posture probably mirrored mine. We were in a life-and-death situation with little time to think of a solution. I thought about taking my foot off the brake and gunning the engine. If I moved quickly around the car in front of us, the man with the gun would have a hard time pulling off a killing shot.

Kenny must have had the same thought, because he began yelling. "Get your foot off the brake!"

But what if the shooter hit one of my children? I couldn't take the chance. I turned to tell Kenny of my dilemma and caught a movement out of the corner of my eye. Behind us, a young man in a suit was laying over the hood of his car. He, too, had a gun and it was pointed straight at my face.

It was just like all the detective stories I had ever read where people say the barrel looked enormous. I still had one foot on the brake and one on the clutch, but I twisted my body until I could throw both screaming children to the floor. I held them down out of range of the gun while Mr. Suit and I continued a stare down.

My entire life flashed through my mind. I was sure it was a sign of my imminent death. Didn't everyone experience such a thing when they were about to die? After a few minutes, I realized the man behind us was hollering something at the man in front. My panicked mind decided the man in front must be a cop and that he was after the man behind us. We must have somehow got caught in the middle and were now being used as some kind of shield. Was the man holding us hostage?

Imagining my face being splattered to smithereens I prayed, *Lord, please don't let my dead body be horrible for Cat and the children to see.*

I've always found it interesting I prayed such a prayer. Did I not have faith enough to ask for deliverance? Or was the situation so impossible I saw no way out? Either way, I sat there expecting that gun to go off any minute.

Kenny was still yelling at me, the engine was still roaring, the man in front of us was yelling something through a megaphone, and the children's wails sounded above it all. "It's no use," I told Kenny. "There's another man behind us with a gun."

Looking behind us, Kenny finally saw the truth of my words and stopped yelling.

At last, I could understand the words coming from the megaphone. "Turn off the engine! Now!"

My first thought was my car was about to blow up. Had someone planted a bomb?

"Now!" The man hollered. "Turn off the engine."

I snapped off the engine. Then I turned back to hold Clay and Jocelyn down on the floor. The man in back was still holding a gun on us.

The man in front continued to yell, holding the megaphone in one hand and a gun in the other. "Get away from the car! Now!"

The squeaking sound of a door opening caught my attention, and I turned in time to see Kenny roll out of the passenger seat and onto the gravel embankment. The look of resignation on his face was terrible to see. It was a mixture of relief and helplessness. Time seemed to stop as I stared upon Kenny's prone body, wondering what he had done to end up in such a place. He was the same age as me and hung out with the same crowd. If I had continued on the same path without giving my life to Christ, would I have ended in the same place?

Sirens suddenly broke the silence. I looked up to see a barrage of police cars appearing from every direction. One car, directly across from me, barely came to a stop before a uniformed man jumped out, aiming a pistol our way. I grabbed a child in each arm and began running down the connecting road, away from the Jeepster, away from Mr. Suit, away from Kenny, away from all the men with guns.

"Halt!" one uniformed man hollered.

"Not on your life!" I hollered back. "Someone's going to get killed!"

Dressed in high heels and a long skirt and carrying two children, I didn't get far before the man stood over me with his pistol pointed at my face. "What's going on here?" he asked.

"You tell me," I said. "You guys are the ones doing everything." I was crying right along with Jocelyn and Clay now; tears streaming down all of our faces.

"You really don't know?" the man asked, but the gun never lowered while we stood there watching the other cops searching my Jeepster and handcuffing Kenny. One policeman was directing traffic, and I realized for the first time the authorities must have held all the traffic back in their search for Kenny. A long line of cars sauntered past, wide eyes staring at my children and me being held at gunpoint. For a moment, I was embarrassed to be seen standing there with tears streaming down my face, but my embarrassment quickly turned to thankfulness. I was alive! Where just moments before I was sure I was going to die.

A policeman soon joined us. "Are you a friend of this man's?" he asked.

"No. I've never met him before in my life. He was a hitchhiker."

"Don't you know better than to pick up hitchhikers?"

"He looked like someone I knew."

"And who would that be?"

It didn't help matters to tell the policeman the hitchhiker looked like Mad Dog. What kind of people have a friend named Mad Dog? He didn't say anything, but his raised eyebrows said it all. Or at least, I thought they said it all. Turned out, his raised eyebrows told another story altogether. But I didn't discover that until three policemen had asked me the exact same questions, pulling every detail possible from me.

My legs were shaking; my arms were weak from holding my children; and my emotions were drained. Finally, I told them I had no more information. No. I was sure I had never seen the man before. No. I didn't usually pick up hitchhikers. No. I wasn't trying to drive him to safety. I was on my way to pick up my son.

Finally, Mr. Suit joined us. "She's answered enough questions," he said.

Just moments before, this man had been threatening my life at gunpoint, now he was speaking in my defense.

"I'm Detective Kennedy," he said. "The man you picked up murdered a guy this morning."

My mouth fell open. "Murdered?"

I looked back to where Kenny was seated in the back of a police car and thought of what could have happened if I had carried a gun or any kind of weapon. He could have used the weapon on my children and me. I thought of how God had changed Cat's and my life and how we could have been in Kenny's place if we hadn't accepted God's grace. My heart went out to Kenny. If he had only known the real life found in Jesus Christ, he could be a free man today, and the guy he killed would be alive.

I came close to being jailed that day. All, but the detective, were convinced I was aiding and abetting a criminal. Detective Kennedy had watched my face and believed I was unaware of my situation. Later, he would question me again to be sure, but in the end they all agreed I had no part in any wrong doing.

Looking back I can see God's protection on our lives that day, yet I am ashamed of the worry and fear that overtook me in the day's before Kenny's trial. Not fear of something real, but fear born of my imagination. I worried about what could happen, the "what if's" of life that paralyze us.

Worry destroys people. A person soon becomes useless and unable to reason things out once they let worry become the ruling force. That's what happened to me, but God reached through all that worry and taught me one of the biggest lessons of my life. He had complete control of my life. He was aware when I picked up the hitchhiker. He knew the outcome. He knew how all the circumstances would follow through. He knew, and He allowed me to go through it all.

Now, I have no need to fear. Jesus is in complete control.

I used to worry about sending my children to someone else's house. I was afraid something bad might happen to them. I was afraid when Cat left for work in the morning, that he might die in a wreck. Fear had ruled my life. Fear of losing the people who meant so much to me.

Now, I am no longer ruled by those fears.

When fear begins to well up and take hold of me, I turn it over to the Lord, knowing He is in control and He knows my every need. This doesn't mean I never fear, but it does mean I know where to go for relief from fear. I don't need to fear the future, because He is in control of the future as well as the past. I have complete trust in Him. I may have never learned such trust if He had not placed me in such an impossible situation.

Shadow of Death
(Based on Psalm 23 and 27)

Yea, though I walk
Through the dark valley of the shadow of death
I will fear no evil, for you are with me
Your rod and your staff, they comfort me

You prepare a table before me
In the presence of my enemies
You anoint my head with oil
My cup is running over
Oh Lord, I know
Your rod and your staff, they comfort me

The Lord is my Light and my salvation
He is my strength, whom shall I fear
Of nothing, shall I be afraid

Oh Lord, my heart goes out
To those behind the darkness
I fear my life may be the only Light they'll ever see
Oh, Lord, let them see your Light in me

The Lord is my Light and my Salvation
He is my strength, whom shall I fear
Of nothing, shall I be afraid

Yea, though I walk
Through the dark valley of the shadow of death
I will fear no evil, for you are with me
Your rod and your staff, they comfort me

Busy

DAYS WERE MORE EXCITING now than they used to be. We had a purpose in life with much work to be done. I taught Sunday School, baked treats for the local Mission, led a youth choir, and visited the sick. My times alone with God were becoming fewer and fewer, but I was sure God would understand. After all, I was busy doing His work.

Endless weeks of activity soon left me feeling exhausted and weak, unable to motivate myself toward any goal. What happened? God seemed so far away. Where was He? Didn't He notice all the work I was doing for Him? I found myself withdrawing and spending more time alone.

Then one morning, I picked up my guitar and began singing my prayers to God. Warm sunshine bathed my face as I sat overlooking the forest where the sweet scent of vanilla joined with birdsong. A feeling came over me then, of rushing wind and lightness of spirit. Utter peace. It felt so good I didn't ever want to leave.

In this state, I began praying for people. Many people I hadn't thought about in a long time came to mind. I ended by praising God for the beauty of His presence. Next I opened up the Word and began to read, discovering the presence of God had been manifested in me through the power of His Holy Spirit. It was the Spirit of God that had brought people to my mind along with their needs.

"This is what I've been missing!" I said aloud. "I've been too busy."

All the work I had been so busy doing for God was from my own motivation and my own strength. It should have been the work of the Holy Spirit in me, then I would have had the strength and motivation needed, and I wouldn't have been left exhausted. The important thing wasn't the work I was doing for God; the important thing was how much of myself I gave to God.

For the first time, I realized God didn't need me to work for Him. What He wanted was my love. If I didn't spend time with Him, then how could I say I loved Him? Loving the Lord with all my heart, all my soul, and all my strength opens the door for everything else to fall into place. Once I discovered this, I kept it as a mantra for my entire life: Love the Lord. Love the Lord. Love the Lord.

Busy
(Based on Psalm 46:10)

I get so busy rushing around
to help the Kingdom come
There seems to be so much work to do
And still so much more to be done
That I miss out when He calls me
When He wants to talk with me
And I don't hear the voice of God
calling out to me

(chorus)
Be still. Be still. Be still my child
Be still. Be still
And know that I am God
That I am God of the universe

I call myself one of His own
I say that Jesus is mine
Yet when He wants to talk with me
I am so hard to find
Cause I'm so busy when He calls me
That I do not hear His voice
Till the still dark hours of the morning
When He calls to me

(chorus)
Be still. Be still. Be still my child
Be still. Be still
And know that I am God
That I am God of the universe

When Peter walked on the water
He kept sight of Jesus' face
It wasn't till he looked elsewhere
That he began to sink in disgrace
Cause he lost sight of the Savior
the one who gave him life
Yet Jesus reached out His arms of love
to lift him up

(chorus)
Be still. Be still. Be still my child
Be still. Be still
And know that I am God
That I am God of the universe

When you find yourself in a hurry
and short of time my friend
Take the time to listen for Jesus
don't lose sight of Him
Keep the door open for Him to enter
Let His light shine through
And listen for the voice of God
calling out to you

(chorus)
Be still. Be still. Be still my child
Be still. Be still
And know that I am God
That I am God of the universe

God

DEPRESSION WEIGHED DOWN ON ME for reasons I didn't understand. Tears would well up for seemingly no reason, and no amount of laughter would coax my heart out of the doldrums. I turned to God, but found no release for the feeling that something was not quite right.

Sleeping through the night brought little comfort. After I sent Cat to work and JayJay and Rob to school, I was waiting for coffee to perk over an open fire, hoping the warmth of both the fire and the coffee would send the coldness inside of me away.

James, a neighbor friend from down the hill, came to visit. He was an older man who spent most of his life on the road. He had many tales to tell, and I always enjoyed his company. He always seemed to "pop" up when I was in trouble and no one else was around to help. Like the time our cow gave birth to her calf in the snow at the far end of our property. Struggling to bring the calf back up to the barn was no easy task, and once it was accomplished I couldn't get the calf to feed from his mother.

There was James, telling me what to do and how to do it and then doing it alongside me. That was his way, and time and time again, he came to the rescue. Yet, today, he was little comfort. I sat on a tree stump holding a warm cup of coffee between my hands, but my mind would not focus on the story James was telling.

The sound of a car engine suddenly caught our attention.

I wasn't expecting anyone and only a few people would try to maneuver our shale road even in summer. I rose to my feet knowing, without understanding how, that I was about to discover the reason for my depression.

Both James and I peered through the forest, waiting for the first appearance of our visitor. When Cat's truck pulled into view, I knew something was very wrong. This was not the time of day he should be returning from work. James and I met Cat halfway as he walked from his truck to our house. When James' eyes met Cat's, he nodded his head and said, "I'll be seeing you two." Then he disappeared in that way of his, here one minute and gone the next.

"What's going on?" I asked Cat.

He opened his mouth to answer, but nothing came out. Instead, he slipped his arm around my shoulders and guided me into the house. Once inside, I turned to face him. "Tell me," I said.

"It's your father."

Instantly, I understood the cause of my depression. It was the Lord's way of preparing me for bad news, but all the preparation in the world would not have helped at that point.

Cat took me in his arms, but I pushed away. "What happened?"

He ran a hand through his hair, keeping his eyes from mine. "Your mother called me at work. Said the doctor told her to call. I'm afraid the news isn't good."

"Is h-he alive?" My voice came out in a croaking whisper.

Cat shook his head and my heart plummeted. "Don't know for sure. He had a massive heart attack. The doctor has him under intensive care, but it took me an hour to get here. By the time we get there—" Cat's voice trailed off.

Without another word, I grabbed my purse and started out the door. Cat was beside me all the way. Silence filled the car as we traveled down our shale road and then sped down the highway, hoping against all odds that Dad would still be alive when we reached the hospital.

I just kept thinking about all the things I had meant to say to Dad. We were a lot alike in our stubborn ways. When I was growing up, we were always in some sort of battle with one another, and it seemed I could never please him. Two particular incidents stood out in my mind from when I was a teenager. The first was when I brought home a report card with straight A's except for one B plus. Dad looked at the card, and the only thing he said was, "What's this B doing on here?"

The second incident happened when I was determined to earn my father's praise. I cleaned the kitchen, scrubbing the walls and even the ceiling. Then I replaced all the shelf and drawer liners and scoured the oven and mopped the floor. When I was sure everything was absolutely perfect, I called for my father.

His inspection took in all the things I had accomplished, and then he stood in the doorway with his eyes circling the room. I was so sure I would finally hear the words, "Well done." But then his eyes stopped at the wall phone. He raised a finger, wiped the top of the phone and held it up for me to see the dust coating it. Then he turned and left the room without saying one word.

From that moment on I gave up trying to please him.

There were other things that happened when I was a teenager; things that were truly wrong. Perhaps I had reason to be hurt and angered by those things, but as I thought of my father lying in that hospital room, I realized how often I had been too selfish to see anything but my own needs. Now, I wanted a chance to tell him how sorry I was for all that resentment. I wanted a chance to tell him above everything that I truly loved him.

But what if death had already claimed him? Would he be with Christ? What about Momma? I had no brothers or sisters, and she was alone in the hospital with either a dead or dying husband. How was she doing even now? The heart attack hit Dad yesterday, what feelings had tortured my mother since then?

Heaviness filled my soul as we continued down the highway in silence. I felt as if I would never be able to move again. I was like a building block dropped into place with the weight of a thousand stones on top.

"Lord," I prayed. "Please help me not to be too late. I'm so, so sorry."

Instantly, perfect peace washed over me, along with a tune, a song with comforting words of hope. My Dad had recently become a follower of Christ. Death would be no loss to him. And the same God who promised victory in death also promised to care for those who were left behind.

That peace stayed with me until we finally reached the hospital where I did get a chance to tell Dad the things I had put off for so long. But when the chance came, the words did not. They weren't needed. Stretching my hand through a thousand tubes running from as many humming machines, I touched Dad's shoulder and captured his eyes with my own. Tears lingered there in my father's eyes—the eyes of a Marine whom I had only seen weep twice before in my entire life.

Words were no longer important. Now we loved as a father and daughter should, and *now* was all that was important.

This Body
(Based on I Corinthians 15 and Philippians 1:21)

(Chorus)
Oh grave where is your victory
Oh death where is your sting
For to me to live is Christ
To die is the greatest gain

This body sown in corruption
Shall be raised in incorruption
This body sown in dishonor
Shall be raised in glory
Sown in weakness
Raised in power
For as in Adam all die
So in Christ
Shall all be made alive
(Chorus)

We shall be like Him
And live forever
We shall be like Him
And live forever
We shall be like Him
And live forever
(Chorus)

Death

DAD HAD DIED during the night, but doctors had worked quickly and skillfully to bring him back with success. He saw God during that time, and the story he has to tell is encouraging and uplifting.

His soul came out of his body, and he crossed over a sea of faces. He could tell they were people lost in darkness without any hope, but he couldn't recognize anyone. It was as if they had lost all identity and were crammed together into a writhing sea of suffering. Then he came to the tunnel described by most people returning from near death experiences. He could see straight through to the other side into a place so beautiful he would later tear up whenever he tried to describe it.

"Oh, the colors there. The colors there," Dad would always say.

Along with the amazing range of colors, Dad felt an enormous peace completely free of fear. There, at the entrance to the tunnel, Dad met a friend whose plane had disappeared a short time before. Rescuers had been searching for the plane for weeks. The two men stood at the tunnel talking while they looked down on the wreckage of the plane. Dad later described how the plane looked and where the bodies would be found.

Searchers found everything exactly as Dad described.

Turning from the wreckage, Dad started through the tunnel with his friend. This time he heard the voice of God say, "You can enter."

"There is no way to describe the grass and everything I saw," Dad told me later. "There's nothing here on earth to compare. I saw the throne of God and a river flowing from the throne. Peace was everywhere."

Dad was about three-quarters of the way through the tunnel when he heard my mother's voice. He turned and saw her praying on the other side of the river. Later, after Dad awoke, and before he talked with anyone, Dad wrote down my mother's prayer word for word. "Please God," he wrote. "If it's not too selfish. Would you please return my husband?"

The words were exactly what my mother prayed when she was in a completely different room of the hospital. Dad heard her praying while he stood there in the tunnel. Then he heard the voice of God answer, "Yes, I will. For a little while."

Immediately, Dad found himself beside my mother in front of a huge congregation with the voice of God speaking through them, telling the younger people to treat the older people better; that we should honor our fathers and mothers; and that we should love one another more and treat one another better.

Then he heard the doctor say, "He's back!"

That experience completely changed my father.

Before, he would always tell me to be sure and plan things out and not to live so haphazardly. After, he said to take one day at a time and not worry about what tomorrow will bring. Before, he battled with a quick temper. After, he was quicker to laugh. Before, he was slow in saying, "I love you." After, the words fell quickly from his mouth.

The biggest thing that plagued Momma was that Dad had not wanted to return to this earth. He said everything was so much better where he had been. Yet he was willing to return for whatever purpose the Lord had for him.

Momma also changed from Dad's experience. Before, she held an enormous fear of death. After, she was no longer afraid. Before, she had always relied on Dad's strength. After, she relied more on a strength and courage that could only come from God.

My family and I discovered a new trust in the sovereignty of God and in His love and protection for us. We learned that He gives us strength to endure hardships as we need it—not a day too early or too late.

Now we are changed people, because of the lessons taught through the experience of death. There is no fear in death for those who belong to God. Each day is a gift to be lived one day at a time, not putting off for tomorrow what should be done today. Because death can claim anyone any time, and not everyone owns the blessed hope of eternal life with Christ.

It Was Not A Dream

By Martha Cowan (for my Dad)

I crossed over the river
Into the Promised Land.
I was carried there by gentle hands.
It was such a beautiful place to see.
A dear friend was waiting there for me.

There were multitudes of people
I did not know,
That didn't matter
It was a beautiful place to go.
This friend of mine was there
He'd gone on ahead.
His family didn't know
If he was alive or dead.

I must tell you he's very much alive.
I saw him there when I arrived.
He showed me where Jesus was near the throne
And said this would soon be my home.

I heard my wife calling to me.
I turned around, God said, "Let it be.
You may go back for a short time
But give them this message of mine.

"Tell others where you've been
And the place I've prepared for them
There are many others who need to know
That this is a beautiful place to go.

"The Word of God they have not been told.
The younger people are neglecting the old.
Each should honor his father and mother
And treat each other as sister and brother.
There should be more love between each one
The way the Father loves His Son.
That love should grow day by day
They should not be turned away."

As I turned to go, my wife was there.
God was answering her prayer.
It brought me back to this life
Perhaps just to be here with my wife.

We really don't know the reason why.
I'm sure we will as time goes by.
I know there is work yet to be done.
I praise the Lord I'm a chosen one.

Dreams

FOR AS LONG AS I CAN REMEMBER I wanted to play the piano. As a young girl, I had visions of myself playing beautiful piano music. Following a trip to the library, I made a paper keyboard and went through two music books, imagining the tunes as I placed my fingers on the proper paper keys. But it wasn't until I was in Junior High School that I was finally able to take piano lessons.

My grandmother rented a piano for me, and my teacher was impressed I was able to go through her first three music books in one lesson—all from what I had taught myself on that paper keyboard! My dreams of being a concert pianist seemed possible at last. But my hopes waned as time passed and my teacher saw no remarkable improvement.

"I'm sorry," she said one day. "You just started too late."

At first her words crushed me, but later I was thankful for the years of lessons that enabled me to enjoy the piano for myself. But one thing I always dreamed of was to be able to sit down at the piano and play music without any written music at all. That seemed like the most awesome thing in the whole world.

Cat did everything he could to make my dream a possibility. Over our years of moving from one place to another, my piano was the first thing he hauled out the door. He did draw the line at hauling it up a flight of steep stairs to our studio apartment over a garage in Eureka, California. Instead, he rolled my piano into the garage, and I could be found there, day or night, playing my favorite tunes. When we moved to the mountain, he waited until summer when the road was dry. Then he hauled the piano onto a truck and up the shale road and rolled it across the floor of what was to be our new home. In a supreme act of love, Cat built the walls around the piano, knowing how much music meant to me.

I had long ago given up my dream of playing without written music, but when some friends invited us to our first Christian concert in Ashland, Oregon, that dream was rekindled. Keith Green was the featured artist. We knew he played piano, so we expected the same church music we heard every Sunday. Were we ever surprised! He played the piano so hard he had to stop halfway through one of his songs to replace one of the keys that had come flying off during his performance. I'll never forget Keith's head of wild curls bent over that grand piano mid concert while he reattached the key.

Keith mesmerized us by singing his heart out—songs he had composed himself—and he used no written music. I felt something stirring deep inside. I could see myself sitting at a piano playing and singing my heart out, just like Keith Green.

The image stayed with me as we listened to his songs and watched people respond to his message of hope. Hard faces softened and sad faces broke into laughter. Every face turned upward when he sang his beautiful love songs to his Creator.

I was beginning to see that music could be used in a multitude of ways. Keith sang songs of testimony about God's work in our lives; songs speaking the very words of God talking to us; songs praising God for His amazing grace; and songs expressing love to an awesome Redeemer. This, to me was the pinnacle of music—to be able to use music as an instrument of prayer. Sure. Books offered prayers set to music. But I still believed the best prayers were from the heart, not from a book.

Later, alone at home, I sat down at the piano and tried playing like I had imagined during Keith's concert. I banged on the piano, singing my heart out, but doing little more than making a very loud noise. When Ron, a neighbor, came up to see if I was in trouble, I gave it up. Ron lived a quarter of a mile away and could hear my banging! What a dumb thing I was trying to do.

The vision forgotten, I returned to playing guitar. At least with that instrument, I could "pray" my songs from my heart. Then one day, something happened that changed everything.

I was listening to Pat Robertson of the 700 Club on our little battery-operated radio. The kids were all in school or taking a nap upstairs. The broadcast featured Thomas Welch, a man known as, "Oregon's Amazing Miracle." He told his story of how he fell off a trestle 55-feet high into a millpond and was under water for nearly an hour! He went into the water a nonbeliever and came out fully trusting Christ. His is an amazing story of complete healing and restoration.

At the end of the program, Pat and Thomas prayed for people. As they prayed, I begged the Lord for the gift of tongues. Tongues was something my own church didn't believe was a valid gift, but I had read how Billy Graham and Corrie Ten Boom (two of my heroes of the faith) had both experienced this gift. If it was good for them, I reasoned, then it would be good for me. So, I had been seeking it but not finding it. While I was praying, Thomas began describing a young woman who was praying for the gift of tongues.

"She's wearing curlers in her hair," he said.

I couldn't believe it! In a day when everyone used curling irons and hair dryers, I had to resort to old-fashioned rollers because we had no electricity. Thomas even described the scarf I was wearing over my curlers. My heart raced. The program was pre-recorded, yet God had placed me on this man's heart even before the fact. Turning up the volume, I listened carefully.

"She thinks she hasn't got the gift of tongues," Thomas was saying to Pat. "But she does. The Lord wants her to know that all she has to do is open her mouth and speak it."

I opened my mouth, but nothing came out.

It hardly mattered. God had heard my prayers. He had placed me on this man's heart. What an incredible thing that the God of the universe pays attention to such detail. I turned off the radio and moved to the A-frame room Cat had made special for me—three walls of windows with my piano on one side, my treadle sewing machine on the other, and a lovely window seat in the middle. I grabbed my guitar and poured out a song of gratefulness to the Living God. To my surprise, another language came out of my mouth. I was singing in tongues. Wow! I sang for several minutes, understanding the meaning of the strange words as I sang and feeling I was reaching deeper than ever before.

Finally, I laid down my guitar and looked longingly at my piano. "Lord," I said. "That piano is such a beautiful instrument. I would sure like to be able to praise you on it."

I heard a voice in my head, very much a command, say, "Do it."

Without questioning, I moved to the piano and played the most beautiful song without faltering for words or music. It is still one of my favorite songs today. I wrote two more songs the same day in praise for the beautiful gift God had given me so freely. I had done nothing at all to deserve it. It was simply a gift of grace, granting the dream of the girl I used to be. I accepted the gift with full joy and vowed in my heart to use it only for the honor and glory of Jesus.

Sunrise

Jesus has given me life
He is everything to me
He is the one who set me free
To be what He wants me to be
In the morning when I need Him most
When the sun just rises over the hill
He fills me with Himself
Like the sun rising in my soul
In the morning will I praise Him
With every breath that is within me
For Jesus is my Lord
And He is the One I love

Let the bells ring
Let the heavens open wide
Jesus has given me life
Let the bells ring
Let the heavens open wide
Pour out your Spirit on your bride

I can see heaven open
I can see my Jesus
Sitting on the right hand of God
I can hear angels singing
I can feel His presence
I can almost see Jesus' face
Thank you Holy Spirit

For revealing Jesus
Thank you for meeting our need
Thank you Holy Spirit
For revealing Jesus
Thank you for giving us life

Let the bells ring
Let the heavens open wide
Jesus has given me life
Let the bells ring
Let the heavens open wide
Pour out your Spirit on your bride

When darkness tries to fill my life
And nothing seems quite right
I lift my hands to Jesus
And He breaks forth
Like the sunrise in my soul
In the morning when I need Him most
When the sun just rises over the hill
He fills me with Himself
Like the sun rising in my soul

Deceived

WHILE DRYING DISHES and listening to Christian radio one day, I heard an interview with a man who had recently moved to Southern Oregon. He said he was associated with Calvary Chapel Costa Mesa and that he was starting a new fellowship in our area. "I'm looking for singers and songwriters," he said.

I nearly dropped the pan I was drying.

For a couple of years I had been sharing my songs with whoever would listen, mostly shut-ins and children, but recently I had been wondering if God wanted me to do more. People in our church encouraged me to look into getting my songs published. Was this radio program God's answer?

I wrote down the phone number and called the man the next time I was in town.

"This is an answer to prayer," Tom said. "Come join us at our next meeting."

He went on to tell me how he was gathering a group of musicians for a traveling ministry. He had already made a record album that was doing very well, and one of the women in his group was a well-known, Christian singer.

Cat was excited for me, but the two of us decided to ask our pastor for his wisdom and advice.

"This won't take us away from our duties here," I assured Pastor Rhea, "because Tom meets at different times than we do here."

Pastor Rhea flashed me an enormous smile. "This is great," he said. "Your songs have touched many hearts here. This group certainly seems to be an answer to prayer."

On our first meeting with Tom, he told us he was a personal friend of Keith Green. This news seemed like further confirmation. Chuck Smith of Calvary Chapel Costa Mesa and Keith Green were two people we very much looked up to as mentors. How wonderful to be associated with one of their friends. So that started our weekend ritual of Saturdays with the musician's fellowship and Sundays with Pastor Rhea.

Saturdays were filled with picnics and baptisms along the Rogue River, young voices lifted in praise to the beat of guitars and hand drums; fresh air filled with the smells of spring grass and spicy scent of oak. Sundays were inside a polished building with hymnbooks, a piano and organ.

I loved the freedom of worship the musician's fellowship brought to us. But after a few months, Cat and I began to notice strange things beginning to happen. Marriages were splitting apart, men were quitting their jobs, and all kinds of rumors began to flow both inside and outside the community. We were torn between staying with the people we had grown to love or with breaking away before we were sucked into something that might lead us astray from walking a good path.

"Did you know," Cat asked me one day, "that Tom listens to Chuck Smith's recordings and then he gives us the exact sermon, word for word?"

Turning to look at him, I struggled for words. "You're sure of this?"

Cat nodded.

That was just one more strange thing to add to our list.

Meanwhile, other people heard we were part of Tom's fellowship and began discussing what to do with us. Instead of coming to us and talking about it, they talked among themselves and passed the information on as a prayer request. People were convinced we would not listen if we were told. We had no idea why we were no longer trusted in our old church. The prayer requests turned into rumors, which soon returned to us.

It was bad enough to feel God had abandoned us by letting us be taken in by this cult; but it was extra painful to have our Christian friends judge us by what they saw on the outside instead of trusting God for our hearts. It seemed to us that our friends in the cult showed us more love and concern than most of the Christians we knew. The few people who finally talked with us did so harshly and came to their own conclusion as to why we had been misled. Their ideas always had to do with us having sinned or acted in rebellion, but I knew we had done nothing wrong. We had even approached our pastor before joining the group.

Confusion became my modifier. The "false prophet" seemed to show us more love than most Christians we knew. I believed with all my heart that most of the cult members were true born-again children of God. Yet, at the same time, I was convinced Tom was not led of God. I wondered why the pastors who knew he was wrong didn't approach him in person.

God didn't answer all my questions right away, but He did give me a beautiful feeling of peace and assurance that He was with me, no matter what anyone else thought.

Then, one day, a friend came right out and told me Tom's fellowship was a cult. "I'm telling you Sandy," Connie said as we were sharing a cup of tea in her living room, "this man is not from God."

"But a lot of people are coming to the Lord," I said.

Connie shook her head, "Doesn't make any difference."

We went back and forth, with her trying to convince me and me insisting she was wrong. Another friend sat wordless on the couch, looking back and forth between us.

Finally, Connie crossed the room to the wall phone and dialed the number for Calvary Chapel Costa Mesa. After a moment, she held out the phone, "Here," she said. "Ask Chuck Smith yourself."

I wouldn't learn until years later, what a miracle it was that she actually got Chuck Smith on the phone. Several thousand people attended his fellowship and he was a very busy man. I took the receiver and slowly brought it to my ear. "Hello," I said.

Chuck responded by saying he heard we were involved with the leader of the musician's fellowship.

"Yes," I said. "He told us he's associated with you."

"Let me tell you about Tom," Chuck said. "Not only is he not associated with us, but we had to bodily remove him from our services. He left a wife and several children down here destitute while he took off to Oregon."

Silence filled the line for several seconds. "But . . . " I finally said, "People are coming to the Lord."

"That is a fruit of the Word," Chuck said. "The Word of God always bears fruit. Now, let me tell you what I see as a fruit of the man's ministry." He went on to name the very things Cat and I had already seen—people so tired they could hardly move, husbands and wives divorcing, men quitting their jobs and refusing to take care of their families. By the time I got off the phone, I wanted to warn all my friends.

Of course, none of our new friends believed us. None of them would even phone Chuck Smith to verify if what I said was true. Then Tom told our friends to have nothing to do with us. "Cat and Sandy have gone to the other side," he told our friends, "and they will suffer for it."

Cat and I pulled away from the group and, as I began to trust God and let Him be the complete authority in my life, my mind began to clear.

I began to recall how tired I had become while attending the musician's fellowship. I remembered one night when it was especially difficult to pick up one foot at a time to walk. It was easier to just sit down and give up. I had seen that same tiredness in some of the people who had been in the fellowship for a long time. They had become so exhausted they didn't have the strength to get away. I came to the conclusion that Tom was dangerously deceived himself. He had become like a wolf in sheep's clothing, seeking to devour God's people, but I couldn't understand how or why.

Later, one of the members of the fellowship ended up in the same women's bible study group as me. For six months, she shared her family's journey of selling their home and all their possessions so they could follow Tom to another country. Everyone in our study group was excited for her . . . except me.

I kept thinking about her four children and how they would probably be left destitute without money or home. I had to warn her! Yet, every time I approached her, she turned a deaf ear to me.

"Call Chuck Smith," I told her one day. "He'll tell you."

Understanding eluded me. My friend knew the Lord. Surely God wouldn't let her be completely misled. Maybe I was just jealous. After all, the group was heading out on a singing ministry—the very thing I had wanted—and I would have been going with them, if we had stayed with the fellowship.

Lord, I prayed. *Please take away any jealousy in my heart, and please take care of this family. Let them be doing the right thing.*

Again, I felt God's peace flow through me, and I approached my friend one more time. "I truly do not believe Tom is led of God," I began. She took a step back, "But I do believe God will honor the right desire of your heart to serve him. I'll be praying for you and your family."

That family, along with many others, ended up losing everything. The leader took the money and disappeared while the others waited in Southern California until they realized Tom would never show up. Through it all, God kept His hand on His people and guided each one through difficult circumstances. Some of my friends are still hurt to this day, but I believe God still holds them in His hands and that one day they will realize His great love.

Looking back, I believe God did have a purpose for my family to be part of the fellowship. Pastor Rhea was right in saying God was leading us. The problem was in me thinking I knew the purpose God had for us there. It wasn't about a music ministry, or even sharing songs; it was about sharing God's love with others and being able to pray for them.

I have learned to not be quite so trusting and to listen carefully to what a person speaks and to test the truth through the Word of God. I don't let so many things "slide" any more, but instead, I pray and speak gently, in love, yet boldly proclaiming the Word of God. I am not saying this is easy or that I do it every time, but it is becoming more a part of my life and I praise God for it.

Early on, bitterness had filled my heart toward the people who had spread rumors about us, yet God removed all that bitterness and showed me how I had done the same thing myself in the past. He showed me through experience how hurtful such actions can be. So, instead of trying to change others, I looked at what needed changing in my own life.

Praise God He used our tough circumstances to teach us to be more aware of what's happing around us and to keep our eyes only on Him, letting Him be the one to reach out and love others through us.

I have repeatedly had to relearn this lesson of looking at my own heart motives. So many times, I have walked through God's open doors with wrong expectations. The amazing thing is God understands. He knows every mistake we are going to make before we even begin, and He uses all things for good. Given enough time, we truly see how He does that, even in the impossibly painful things.

All You Want

(Based on Isaiah 40:6-9 & 2 Corinthians 4:18)

Lord, help me to see
That all you want of me
Is to love you
With every breath I breathe
To try and find the words
To praise you

Lord, help me to see
Your face always before me
And when the darkness comes
The night is all around me
Help me, Lord, to see
Your face shining through
And not look on a man
Who's as the grass
And the flower of grass
That shall fade and pass away
Here today
And gone tomorrow

Oh Lord, help me to see
Your face always before me
And when the darkness comes
The night is all around me
Help me, Lord, to see
Your face shining through
And not look on a man

Lord, help me to see
Your face always before me
And when the darkness comes
The night is all around me
Help me, Lord to see
Your face shining through

Treasure

IT WAS ROUND AND SHINY. Dad had given it to me when I was just a little girl, telling me to keep it with me always for good luck. He joked about how I would never be completely broke as long as I had that silver dollar. It was special to me because Dad had won it in Reno, Nevada, and had brought it all the way home for me.

Through the years, whenever I would open my wallet and see the silver dollar inside, I couldn't help but think of my father. It was like a link between him and me even when we were thousands of miles apart. In the years when I grew rebellious and only thought of the bad times growing up, the silver dollar would remind me of good times so easily forgotten.

Now it was gone. I had left my wallet in a restaurant, and when I returned to retrieve it, it was missing with my silver dollar inside—my silver dollar, which was now worth a good deal more than a dollar. Only a very honest person would return it.

Saddened by the loss of my father's gift, I asked God to let me find my purse, reminding Him it wasn't the money that was important but the remembrance embracing many years, a remembrance that couldn't be replaced.

Not long after my prayer, I received a call from the Police Department. "Are you missing a wallet?" The dispatcher asked.

"Yes!" I nearly screamed into the phone, excited that God had answered my prayer.

Driving down to the police station, I thought of how nice it was that honest people still existed. I nearly skipped up to the reception desk. She called for an officer to bring my wallet. After a long wait he entered, carrying my wallet with him.

Yes! It was mine.

He handed the wallet to me, and I opened it. *Empty.* No silver dollar. No money. But my driver's license was still inside.

Feeling foolish, I looked up at the officer who was explaining that my purse was discovered in a men's restroom at a service station.

"Thanks," I said, barely lifting my head. "It's good to have my driver's license, and I'm sure glad I don't own any credit cards."

As my footsteps clattered across the stone floors, I began to feel resentment and not just a little stupid and naïve at being so optimistic as to think there were honest people in the world. *God,* I whispered. *I know this isn't a big thing, but I thought you cared about the little things as well as the big. I guess I'm just not important to you after all.*

Returning home, I realized my feelings were silly and not at all what they should be, but it's one thing to know you're doing something wrong; doing something about it is another thing altogether. I battled with my feelings, realizing the issue was much bigger than losing a mere silver dollar, remembrance or not. The question was, did God care or didn't He?

If God is God over all, then He can handle the little things as well as the big things. There couldn't possibly be too much for Him to do. He said He cared about us, enough to die for us, enough to know the number of hairs on our heads, enough to provide for our needs, and to give us gifts even our earthly fathers wouldn't give. Then why did He let me down? I knew He was capable of taking care of the situation, but He chose not to. Why?

Finally, going to the Word of God, I found the answer. Certain verses began to stand out to me, such as Matthew 6:19-21, *"Do not store up for yourselves treasures on earth, where moth and rust destroy, and where thieves break in and steal. But store up for yourselves treasures in heaven, where moth and rust do not destroy, and where thieves do not break in and steal. For where your treasure is, there your heart will be also."*

Could it be I was guilty of being attached to earthly treasures? Me? A mother who lived in a house with no inside walls, no running water, no inside plumbing, no chandeliers or tiled floors?

But how about the pictures hanging on my walls that Cat had painted and I loved so much? And my piano? And how about all those handmade things that had been given to me, my photo albums, baby books, first set of dishes, favorite dress and, of course, my silver dollar?

Lord, I prayed, *please forgive me. I have been selfish. I have placed earthly things in too high a position. You asked me to love you with all my heart, soul, and mind, and to store up treasures not made on this earth. Yes, Lord, I have loved this earth, this home of ours, so peaceful in the trees. Watching the sunrise in the morning. Sitting in the warmth of it as it comes over the hill. Listening to the birds and squirrels instead of the noise of car engines. Being able to hear leaves dropping from trees. Being able to feel close to you at any moment, not feeling rushed or pressured.*

"No. I have not been willing to give this up. Telling myself you would never want me to leave this place, knowing I could never be happy anywhere else. Please forgive me, Lord, and give me the desires you want me to have. Thank you, Lord."

Little did I know then, that it was the great mercy of a loving God that took a silver dollar to help prepare me for the loss of every material treasure I had ever owned. For within a month, our house in the woods, burned to the ground with everything in it. Yet, because of the lesson learned through the silver dollar, I no longer had my eyes on these earthly treasures, but was grateful for the treasures I had stored where moth and rust cannot destroy. Grateful for the safety of our family, knowing God did care about the big things as well as the little things and that He was in full control.

Where Your Treasure Is
(Based on Matthew 6:19-20)

(Chorus)
Where your treasure is
There your heart will be
Where your treasure is
There your heart will be
Where your treasure is
There your heart will be
Where is your treasure

Don't store your treasure on earth
Where moth and rust can destroy
And thieves break in and steal
You will have them no more
Where is your treasure
(Chorus)

Store up your treasure in heaven
Where moth and rust cannot destroy
And thieves can't take away
You will have them forever
Where is your treasure
(Chorus)

Preparation

IT WAS A BUSY DAY. Our three youngest children were in bed for a nap, including Michelle who was home from school with a head cold. After rearranging my kitchen, I stopped to admire it. The new shelves added a special touch and the counters were clean and gleaming. The smell of smoke kept bothering me, but I thought it must come from the brushfire on the hill above, because each time I stepped outside to look, I found nothing out of the ordinary.

While I surveyed our cozy home, my thoughts drifted back over the years and all the changes our house had come through.

We started out with two rooms and no roof or ceiling. How scared I used to get when Cat left to work the night shift at a lumber mill. After the sun would go down, I would light the kerosene lanterns and listen to my battery-operated radio, bringing the outside world a little closer. We had no phone or computers in those days, no front or back door, and no roof. A chest of drawers covered the back entrance, and another covered the front. I worried about Big Foot and mountain lions, and other strange creatures that might be creeping through the forest at any moment to carry my children and me away.

I had been too long in the city and too disconnected from my beloved forest. It would take years to relearn the skills of my childhood and the fearlessness of my youth.

On this particular night, my dog sat at my feet comforting me with her protection while the children were sleeping in their beds. Strange noises sounded from the darkened forest and I had visions of the children and myself disappearing with no one ever knowing what had happened to us.

While thinking these thoughts, an enormous beetle flew in, attracted by the fumes from the kerosene lantern. It sounded like a buzz bomb. I had never seen anything like it before. It was nearly as big as my hand!

Missy, our protective elkhound thought the beetle was a fun play partner. As soon as it landed, she ran over and bumped it with her soft paw. Up it went, buzzing and flying straight for me. I screamed and pulled a blanket over my head. My only thought was to get out of there and away from the bug, but I couldn't find the door with the blanket over my head. Whenever the buzzing stopped, I would hear Missy running across the wood floor. Then the buzz would start again. Each time the bug hit my blanket, I screamed in terror. The children remained in their beds, but I didn't see how they could sleep through my screaming.

Soon, I heard knocking at my door.

"Come in."

I peeked through a tiny gap in my blanket to see who would appear. It was Ron, our nearest neighbor from a quarter mile away, coming to my rescue.

"I heard screaming," he said, so I brought my shotgun."

Feeling braver, I pulled the blanket back and searched the room. The beetle had come to rest on the wall across from us. I pointed at it.

Ron looked at the beetle and then back at me. "You, uh, want me to shoot it?"

"Probably not," I admitted. "It would be hard to explain to Cat how the hole got in the wall."

"Yeah," Ron agreed, squinting his eyes.

I handed him a big book. "This should do it," I said.

He smacked the beetle with a horrible crunch.

"Is it poisonous?" I asked.

"Nah." He shook his head. "Harmless wood beetle. They hardly ever show themselves."

When he left, I settled down to listen to the night sounds. Two more beetles flew in that same night. The third one was so big I ran out of the house and stayed in the car until Cat came home. Dad had always told me that if you didn't show fear, then things wouldn't hurt you—things like mean chickens and big bugs—so I believed my children were safe in their comfortable beds. But just in case, I kept my ears pealed for any blood curdling shrieks.

When Cat returned home in the wee hours of the morning, he found the children sleeping comfortably in their beds with their mother nowhere to be found. Finally, discovering me fast asleep in the car, he couldn't help but remark on my bravery, or lack thereof. After searching the house for any more beetles, we settled down for a good night's sleep. I could face anything as long as Cat was beside me.

Following nights, afraid our lanterns might attract other strange creatures, I sat in the dark in our roofless house until Cat returned home,.

The first winter about killed us. We finally had a roof, but no ceiling or inside walls. Cat had lost his job at the lumber mill and I was pregnant with our fourth child, so money was scarce.

One night, it grew so cold inside our house that a two-gallon bucket of water froze solid.

Cat left every morning to work off our bill at the hospital, taking JayJay and Rob with him on their way to school. I couldn't keep a fire going in our cheap wood heater while snow piled up outside. Four-year-old Michelle and I would huddle in bed with the covers wrapped tightly around us and our teeth chattering until Cat returned home to warm us up with a good roaring fire. Even then, we had to sit very close to the heater to feel any warmth.

When the second winter came along, we felt more prepared. More families had moved to the mountain, and we would often get together for dinner and help each other whenever needed. It was a good feeling to know help was nearby. We had grown to two rooms in our home, with a sleeping loft for JayJay and Rob. Plastic sheets made a temporary ceiling, which kept the heat down near the floor where we needed it most. I had an indoor sink with a 55-gallon drum taking in water from our rain gutters.

A friend moved in with us, sleeping on the couch and helping with chores and carrying groceries up the hill from our car. That trek was something I always hated. All groceries and supplies had to be carried a quarter mile up hill through clay mud that kept sticking to our shoes until it seemed as if we carried ten extra pounds on our feet. The bags would get wet and break, and Michelle would cry to be carried. We would return home to a bitterly cold house, leaving everyone grouchy and with no warm water to wash away the mud.

Everywhere we went, we carried some of that red, sticky mud with us. Most of the time, we would remove our shoes before entering a building, but often it was impossible. I'll never forget the time we went to a Laundromat that featured working attendants. Their machines had a prewash cycle. I was sure a prewash was the only thing that would even begin to remove the mud and soot from our clothes.

We entered the Laundromat with three muddy children and a baby. Cat carried in boxes of clothing, which also had mud on the bottoms and set them in front of the machines. When all the boxes were finally inside and all the children shoeless, Cat walked to the carpeted sitting area to read a magazine while he waited for me. His logging boots left tracks right across the middle of the room.

One of the attendants came running. "Just look at this mud! You can't be sitting here."

Cat stood.

The attendant grabbed a chair and placed it next to the washing machine where I was loading clothes. "You'll have to sit here," she demanded. "And try not to walk around."

It was comical watching my long-legged husband sitting like a brick with women and laundry carts dodging all around him. But bitterness began to grow inside our hearts—bitterness toward people who took no time to understand. That's why we moved to our country home in the first place.

I grew up as an only child in a generation that believed their parents loved them, no matter how strong or how unwarranted the discipline. We were taught that justice would always be served. This gullibility left me unprotected against people who took advantage of such things. At the same time, my entire generation began to question most of the things our parents had taken for granted. I felt cheated to learn many things weren't what they seemed. Justice wasn't always meted out and terrible things happened behind closed doors. The Leave-it-to-Beaver (a popular sitcom at the time)families weren't always what they appeared to be.

I had no one to turn to when things went wrong at home. No safe house. No caring counselor. No kind social worker.

Cat was his own person from a very young age. He was a terror to his mother, which left him feeling her loathing. Bitterness grew. On the day he left for Vietnam to fight a war that was never called a war, she said, "I love you as a son, but I hate you as a person."

Those words turned Cat into a very angry person.

Cat and I met when my marriage of six years ended in divorce and Cat was disillusioned and empty after several meaningless affairs. Together we would win the world. Together we got off the hold of drugs and booze. Together we found the meaning of real love.

We always felt out of place with everyone else.

We didn't quite fit the groove of the free-loving, peace-proclaiming hippy and wanted nothing to do with the shortsighted, biased, redneck (as we saw them). So, we searched for our rainbow's end and found it in this, our home in the woods, with no one nearby to judge or question our choices.

Then Christ changed our lives completely. He replaced our confusion with peace and gave us a reason for living. He filled us with His love, which helped us to love others, even those who didn't love us in return.

We were unburdened and free, basking in our newfound faith and freedom . . . totally unsuspecting of the trauma to come.

The Living God
(From Daniel 6:26-27)

(Chorus)
For He is the Living God
And He endures forever
His kingdom will not be destroyed
His dominion will never end
He rescues and He saves
He provides great signs and wonders
In the heavens and on the earth

He rescued Daniel from the lions
He brought his children cross the Red Sea
He gave the song to King David
And He is more than able to rescue me

For He is the Living God
And He endures forever
His kingdom will not be destroyed
His dominion will never end
He rescues and He saves
He provides great signs and wonders
In the heavens and on the earth

When I lost my way and grew weary
He strengthened my feeble arms and weak knees
He provided a level path for my feet
He is more than able to rescue me

For He is the Living God
And He endures forever
His kingdom will not be destroyed
His dominion will never end
He rescues and He saves
He provides great signs and wonders
In the heavens and on the earth

Fire

GOD, PLEASE! I prayed one day. *Give me a house with running water, and a nice road that doesn't beat us to death.*

He spoke to me then, in the recesses of my mind and heart. *Be content, child, with what you have. Then I will grant your request.*

Those words sent me on a quest to be a thankful person. I purposed in my heart to only see the good in things and ignore the bad. I tried to tell myself, *Mud doesn't matter.* But tears filled my eyes after a half-mile hike to the car where I discovered all of us were covered with the sticky substance. I tried to tell myself it didn't matter that I didn't have linoleum or carpet. I would remind myself that many people survived under much worse circumstances. But the more I tried to be content, the more discontent I seemed to become.

Finally, in desperation, I cried, "God, I want to do what you want me to do. I truly do! But I don't have the strength to do it."

I felt I had failed at the Christian life, that I was unable to accomplish the small thing God had asked of me. But then, strange things began to happen.

Someone gave us a new wood heater for our living room. It actually kept us warm, Another friend gave us a porcelain sink set in a cabinet with drawers and doors. Someone else gave us a big 750-gallon tank to replace our 55-gallon drum. Now, we hardly ever had to haul water. Cat bought new tires for our pickup that enabled us to drive right up to our house. No more trudging through the wet mud. Someone gave us carpet that ended up covering our floor from wall-to-wall in our living and sitting rooms. Cat's Dad gave us a wood cook stove for the kitchen, which was a tremendous help in heating water and keeping the upstairs warm. Then the most amazing gift of all . . . electricity!

One of our neighbors paid to have power poles service our entire community. We couldn't afford to wire our entire house, but Cat made an outside shed where we stored a refrigerator and freezer. Then he brought one electric line into the house where we could plug in a few things at a time . . . an electric blanket, the stereo, a lamp. I soon forgot about how much I had wanted to move away.

Now, five days before Thanksgiving, I surveyed our cozy home while our three children were still taking their naps. I had just finished cleaning, and our home looked perfect. The kitchen was gleaming and the smell of fresh-baked Snickerdoodles filled the air. Our canary was singing happily in his cage, my piano gleamed with a new coat of lemon oil, and sunlight poured through the windows of our living room, making it look like an old-fashioned painting. Flickering flames in our cast iron fireplace made the entire scene look like a classic painting.

Most everything in our house was homemade—Cat's paintings hanging on the walls, the painted flowerpots siting on the windowsills, Cat's sculptures, my hand-braided rugs and the quilts on our beds. The house itself was homemade with an inscription on one of the beams, "Cat and Sandy Cathcart, May 1, 1973."

I thought about how God had taken the circumstances I had hated and how He changed them in such a way I was now completely content. *God,* I prayed, *you truly do care about every area of our lives, and it's clear you know the desire of our hearts. Thank you.*

I barely finished my prayer when a scream shattered the stillness. "Mom!"

Clay was calling for me at the top of his lungs. I ran up the stairs where I found Clay and Michelle staring at a wall of flames.

I scooped up Jocelyn from her crib and handed her to Michelle. "Get out!" I said. "Get away from the house, and stay out."

I grabbed a quilt off the bed and turned to Clay, who was still staring at the burning wall. "Out!" I commanded. "Go with your sister."

Then I threw the quilt over the flames, trying to smother the fire as I had seen in movies. I was heartbroken to lose the quilt that had taken me a year to make, but it seemed worth it as smoke filled my nostrils and the flames disappeared. Relief washed through me. And then, poof! The quilt was suddenly aflame!

I threw another quilt on top of the first and beat it with my hands, thinking of the repair work all this was going to take— the wall and floor and quilts. Again, the fire seemed to die. And then, poof! The second quilt was in flames.

After the third quilt, I gave up trying. The fire had now grown into something that seemed impossible to stop. I turned, planning to run downstairs and see what water I could find, but Clay and Michelle were still standing there, wide-eyed and open-mouthed. I lifted Jocelyn from Michelle's arms and led them outside to a safe spot where I had them sit. "Do not move from here," I said, as I placed Jocelyn in Michelle's lap.

Grabbing the only bucket of water I could find, I ran back into the house and up the stairs. Then I pulled back the bucket and gave it a mighty heave, throwing a wave of water over the burning wall.

Smoke immediately filled the burning room and I broke out in a coughing fit. This couldn't be happening. I needed help. But what could I do? I had no car, no telephone, no water.

I hurried back downstairs, thinking I should retrieve some things, but as I stood in the living room, everything suddenly seemed too important and too big.

Smoke and flames were still contained upstairs. Down here the air was clear and nothing seemed amiss. I stood staring at my piano with a rush of memories flooding through me. That piano was my first, and it had traveled with me from the time I was a young teenager. Could I push it through the wall? Of course not.

I remembered having a plan in case of fire, but the plan eluded me.

Something broke within me then and all I could do was turn around in confusion. "No God. No God," I cried.

When I look back on that moment, I often think how close I came to death. I would have still been standing there turning in circles, crying out to God, and convincing myself it was all just a bad nightmare, if God hadn't intervened. But He did . . . and in a most unusual way.

Smokey, our house cat, ran across the floor in front of me, frantically trying to find a way out of the house. I immediately snapped out of my confusion and knew what to do.

Rescue the cat!

I chased down Smokey and gathered him in my arms. On my way out, I gabbed my guitar case, a bible, my purse, and

Michelle's coat, all things that were within an arm's reach. I carried them outside and dropped them on the ground.

Smokey streaked off into the forest.

When I turned to reenter the house, the sight that met my eyes stopped me. The upstairs windows had completely melted and flames were reaching high into the sky. Trees near the house were getting dangerously hot, and I suddenly realized a forest fire could break out any moment. When an explosion sounded from somewhere deep in the house, I knew I could not return into that inferno.

I had to get my children to safety.

None of the children were wearing shoes, so I carried Jocelyn while Clay and Michelle picked their way carefully across the rocky road. It was slow going as we dropped into the canyon and back up the other side. When we reached the big road, we turned and looked back. Flames rose above the tall timber and I feared we were still in danger. It had been a very dry season.

We hurried on, hoping to reach a neighbor's house before everything was lost, or at least before fire swept through the surrounding forest. But the children's feet were tender and our going was painfully slow. No one was home at the first house, or the second. We had already walked a half-mile, and the next house was over a mile away down the shale road. My throat ached from inhaling so much smoke, I felt dizzy and sick, and my arms were tired from carrying Jocelyn. All three children were crying. They would never make it over that next mile with bare feet.

I dropped to the ground in front of Kenny's house, joining my children in their tears, the three of us clinging to one another. "God!" I cried. "How could you let this happen?"

The sound of a car engine brought all our heads up. We stood to our feet as we saw Omar, a German immigrant who lived with Kenny, come into view. We waved our arms and flagged him down, but he had a difficult time deciphering the English words of an hysterical woman and three crying children.

"Break into Kenny's house. No problem," he said. "There is phone."

Then Omar turned his car around and sped away. I called for him to return, but he never heard me. I was sure he must have a key, but I watched our only hope of rescue fly down the mountain in a cloud of dust. Through the opened car windows we could hear Omar yelling, "Fire! Fire!"

My heart sank.

We searched Kenny's house, but the only window that wasn't too high was too small for Michelle or me to crawl through. Could I trust a five-year-old to open the door for us?

I sent Clay through with specific instructions and he followed them perfectly. Soon, I was on the phone calling the Forestry Department and explaining our plight. They promised to send someone, but I knew it would be too late to save any of our possessions. Still, I hoped for some kind of miracle and that they could stop the fire from spreading through the forest. Finally, I called Cat at work. He was away, driving truck, so I had to leave a message.

When I hung up the phone, Kenny came through the door. "Omar told me what happened," he said. "How bad is it?"

"Very," I said. "It may have reached the forest by now."

Kenny looked up the hill. "You stay here. I'll go check."

He soon returned with the good news that only one tree was on fire, and the bad news that the house was completely gone. "Leave the children with me," he said, "and you go wait for the forestry truck."

I did as he said, sitting alone on a boulder, waiting for someone to appear. What on earth would we do? We had no insurance and less than ten dollars in the bank. We still owed money on the land.

When the sound of a motor reached my ears, I was surprised to see my husband appear. There was still no sign of the Forest Service vehicle. Cat scooped me up in his arms for a quick hug before driving me back to the house. I expected to see it still burning, with flames coming out every window. Nothing prepared me for the reality.

Our house was completely gone.

It had burned to the ground with everything in it. Nothing was recognizable. Both cast iron stoves had melted into enormous globs of metal. It looked like a huge burning bonfire.

Cat rushed to his motorcycle. The leather seat over the gas tank was on fire.

"No!" I hollered.

Ignoring me, Cat pulled off his shirt and began beating out the flames. Then he moved his motorcycle to safety. Next, he ran for the burning shed that held our refrigerator and freezer. It was a simple frame with a roof and no walls. Cat pushed the refrigerator through the frame and onto the hard ground. The force of it caused him to lose his balance. As he struggled to regain his feet, the freezer exploded.

"Cat!" I yelled. "Please, don't take any more chances."

He came over to me then and held me in his arms. Together we watched our dreams go down in flames, but surprisingly we shed no tears. I remembered the loss of my silver dollar and how God had used that loss to show me what was important in life. My house was gone—all of my family heirlooms, my piano, Cat's paintings and sculptures, our photo albums and baby books— every earthly treasure. But I had my husband and children, the only treasures I could truly take into eternity with me.

Standing there in Cat's arms I felt nothing but gratitude.

That's how the Forest Service personnel found us, personnel that consisted of one man in a pickup truck carrying two 55-gallon drums of water.

"I'm not allowed to put out the fire," he said apologetically. "I can only keep the fire from spreading into the forest."

No wonder he had taken his time in getting here. For the next few hours, he stayed with us, sharing in our tragedy. He remarked several times how astounding it was that we weren't falling apart. He said he had never seen anything like it.

"We have what's important to us," Cat said. "Our lives and our faith."

The man just shook his head in amazement.

We heard the sound of another car engine and were surprised to discover Suzy, a dear friend, who had overheard the phone call I had made to Cat. She had picked up JayJay and Rob on their way home from school—another gift from God. She told the boys what had happened before they reached the scene, sparing them the shock of seeing the house without knowing what was going on.

"You come to our house when you're finished here," she said. "All of you."

"But—" I started.

She shook her head. "No but's about it. We have plenty of room."

She left JayJay and Rob with us and promised to pick up our other three children on the way down the mountain. "I'll give them dinner," she said. "And there will be plenty of food waiting for you."

Later, after the fire had cooled to glowing embers and everyone else had left, Cat gathered JayJay, Rob, and me together to pray. It was a clear, moonless night with millions of stars shimmering in the sky.

We joined hands as Cat prayed. "Lord, you have our attention now. We are trusting you to lead us in the way you would have us go. Thank you for keeping us all safe."

We stood there, taking one last look at the charred remains of our dream home. Everything we owned on earth was destroyed. Many things that had been in the family even before we were born, were now gone. Gladness filled my heart that Jesus was our greatest treasure, and nothing could ever take Him away. He is the Alpha and Omega, the beginning and the end. When heaven and earth are gone, He will still remain, and we shall be with Him.

We turned to go, not in despair, but in trust that God was working a miracle in our lives.

Give Me The Mountain

I see a mountain, blue skies above
Streams flowing, birds singing
I see a valley with hot city streets
And people rushing everywhere

(Chorus)
Give me the mountain and I will be free
Give me the valley, I'll tell others of you
I'd take the mountain, Lord, for the feeling I would feel
But the valley is where I will be

What if you, Lord, had refused to come
To leave the pleasure of your heavenly home
We'd still be lost today with no purpose in life
No hope for a world without you
(Chorus)

I know someday, Lord, that I will be with you
On that mountain where I long so to be
But till that day, Lord, I'll walk this valley
Knowing you are the Light that shines through me
(Chorus)

Epilogue

GOD DID WORK A MIRACLE in our lives, but it wasn't one that was worked overnight. We went through times of deep despair and frustration. There was even one time I told God He had done what He said He wouldn't do. That He had given me more than I could take. But He hadn't, for at that very moment He was providing a "way out."

It would take a whole book to write down the miracles and lessons learned after the fire, but the number one thing was how important the Word of God became in our lives. God answered every hurt, every frustration, and even my anger so directly through His Word that often I felt ashamed for having doubted. Then He would even take care of my shame and fill me anew with His strength and power to make it through.

I remember one particular time when I wanted so badly to run away. It was all I could do not to take the money we had saved since the fire and get in the car and go . . . anywhere, didn't matter where . . . just away. I knew it was the wrong thing to do, but the urge was powerful, and tears just flowed and flowed. Seemed they would never stop.

I knew God was telling me to go to His Word, but I didn't want to. I didn't even want to talk to Him. But He gently kept persisting until I broke down and went to Him in prayer. I was so totally "out of it" that I felt as though someone else was in control of my body and I was just going through the motions.

The first thing God led me to do was take a shower. So I did, a nice long one, until I could finally feel my body responding. Then I dressed and read God's Word.

I could not believe what I read . . .

> In repentance and rest is your salvation,
> in quietness and trust is your strength,
> but you would have none of it.
> You said, "No, we will flee on horses."
> Therefore you will flee!
> —Isaiah 30:15-16 (NIV)

That's exactly how I had felt! I read on and came to verse 18 . . .

> Yet the Lord longs to be gracious to you;
> He rises up to show you compassion.
> For the Lord is a God of justice.
> Blessed are all who wait for Him!
> —Isaiah 30:18 (NIV)

I could imagine the Lord rising to His feet to show me compassion as I refused Him and kept going my own way. I could sense the longing in His heart for me to return to Him.

Laying down my Bible, I stilled before the Living God, thanking Him for His great mercy and for not giving up on me.

Then I finished reading the passage. It is still a favorite of mine. Circumstances did not immediately line up, but I was now relying upon God's strength instead of my own, and I was placing my trust in Him.

We now have a beautiful home with more and better "earthly" things than we had before the fire. I was even given a piano! We have more opportunities for ministry than ever before, and our lives are filled with purpose.

There are times, though, when I really miss the quiet and peace of the mountain. Those are the times I find a place to sit still before the Lord and dwell upon His promises . . . even if it means sitting on the edge of the bathtub. I'm finding it takes a higher commitment, a real act of the will, to make time to spend in the Word of God and in prayer amidst all the interruptions of modern life. But such time is vital to our growth as Christians.

We now have a beautiful relationship with Cat's parents. It's nice to know that even the deepest wounds can heal. God living in us can bring forgiveness that we would otherwise be incapable of expressing. He replaces bitterness with love.

I leave you now with the assurance that God is reaching out to you. We are the ones who turn our backs on Him and refuse to give Him our time.

In repentance and rest is your salvation.
In quietness and trust is your strength.
—Isaiah 30:15 (NIV)

It is a daily commitment of our lives to God that will bring about a daily miracle of life in our innermost beings.

If He Came Back Today

If He came back today
Would you see Him standing there
Would you recognize His voice
When He whispers in your ear
Or would you be too busy
Doing all the things you do
Day after day

Do you recognize His smile in the sunrise
Across the land
Do you know His touch when He heals you
With His hand
Do you know His truth to free you
From all your worldly gain
Day after day

(Chorus)
Day after day, He calls you by name
Day after day, He is always the same
In the unexpected places, and in unexpected ways
Day after day, He calls you by name

His peace is a river flowing
Through your mind
His love is a blanket around you
All the time
His arms are like a refuge
A place to hide away
Day after Day

He's there in the tears of our children
When they cry
He's found in the wonder of all
Their questions, "Why"
He calls out oh so tenderly
In a hundred million ways
Day after Day

A Word From The Author

I wrote this book 35 years ago, long before I considered myself an author. I've left it pretty much the way it was. I think there is something in the simplicity of the writing that matched my newfound faith. I had only been walking the Jesus Way for five years.

Now, I've been walking with Jesus for forty years!

What an incredible and exciting journey this has been. And I hold the hope of eternity walking this amazing journey with Jesus.

Back when I was a new believer, sharing my songs in front of the congregation, I would often share that I thought it was really a pretty easy thing to live the Christian life. God only required two things of us: to love Him and to love others.

The word "Christian" has since lost it's true meaning as a follower of Christ. Because of this, I rarely use the term. It is not Christ who has changed; He remains the same, it is our perception of the word "Christian" that has changed. It has become synonymous with bigot and political parties, with rules and pointing fingers, things that have nothing to do with Christ.

My Native American friends who walk with Jesus describe this journey as walking in Beauty, or walking the Jesus Way.

Now, forty years later, I still claim that walking the Jesus Way is really an easy thing to live out. His commandments are still the same—love God and love others.

That's all there is to it!

We can spend the rest of our lives learning to love God, and He sets His Spirit within our hearts to help us accomplish that very thing. When we truly love God, it becomes an easy thing to love others, because we see them the way He does. And we find ourselves wanting to please Him by walking in His steps.

Today, you will often hear me say that the Christian life is counterintuitive, meaning it doesn't come natural. Our natural bent is to lean on our own understanding. The Jesus Way says lean not on your own understanding, but in all your ways acknowledge God and He will direct your paths.

The natural way says I deserve something. The Jesus Way says we deserve condemnation and judgment, and that's exactly why Jesus gave His life in exchange for our condemnation and judgment, He gives mercy and grace to all who will receive it.

The natural way says humans are basically good, even when we look around at our crazy world and see that is utterly false. The Jesus Way says we fail without Him, but we win through Spirit life.

The natural way says to find myself. The Jesus Way says to lay myself down. It is in dying to my self that I discovered who I was truly created to be—a child of the Most High God, created to be holy and blameless in His sight!

I never thought I could be a faithful person, but through walking the Jesus Way, I have been faithful to my Creator, my husband, and my family. Through sadness and sorrow, through joy and loss, I have discovered my Creator Redeemer is forever trustworthy and faithful.

My life is a song rescued from the deepest night.

I Stand Amazed

All that I am I surrender
All that I claim is now yours
All that I ask is forever
Forever and always I stand

(chorus)
I stand amazed in the power of your presence
I stand amazed in the strength of your grace
I stand amazed in the light of your glory
Forever and always, I stand amazed

Your love amazing has filled me
Your light has given me hope
Your Word forever will guide me
Forever and always I stand

I stand amazed in the power of your presence
I stand amazed in the strength of your grace
I stand amazed in the light of your glory
Forever and always, I stand amazed

By day the Lord directs His love,
at night His song is with me—
a prayer to the God of my life.
—Psalm 42:8 (NIV)

Visit

---

www.needlerockpress.com
for future books!

www.sandycathcartauthor.com
for Sandy's blog and updates

www.sandycathcart.com
for Sandy's Art & Photography

www.restoringtheheart.com
for Native American Insight

www.ghostdancershadley.com
for Daily Inspiration

Contact

SANDY CATHCART is a freelance writer, photographer and artist, as well as a scribe for Restoring The Heart Ministries. She lives in the High Cascades of Southern Oregon with her husband, The Cat Man, where she writes about Creator and everything wild.

Sandy loves hearing from her readers.
You can find her on Facebook:
https://www.facebook.com/sandycathcartauthor/

You can also email her at:
sandy@sandycathcartauthor.com

Request

Reviews are like gold to authors.
If you have enjoyed reading this book
would you please consider leaving a review
at Amazon or Goodreads
and tell your friends about it!

Thanks very much!

What People Are Saying About Needle Rock Press Books

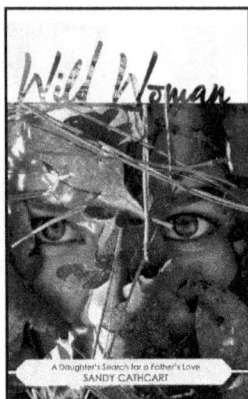

Praise for *Wild Woman: A Daughter's Search For A Father's Love*

From an Oregon Reader

"This book made me do something I don't believe I've ever done with a book before. When I finished it, I immediately went back to the beginning and started reading it again. And found new gems of wisdom the second time."

From an Amazon Reader

"How many times does the enemy of our soul whisper lies into the silence of our minds about those we love or care for? Lies that are born of misunderstandings brought on by imaginings of what we "think" our loved ones say or don't say. How many wasted hours, days or years are spent in anger over words said in a moment of exhaustion, frustration, or disappointment?

"Sandy's story is a beautiful example of what our Creator and Redeemer longs to do in each of us through forgiveness and love. When we allow him to do that in us, we suddenly become free to be loved and to give love, as he heals our broken hearts and restores to us lost relationship."

From an Amazon Reader

"This is a woman who loves the wilderness and is at home in it. She brings you the scents of campfires and forest earth, and the love of the God she calls Creator Redeemer."

Praise for *Shaman's Fire (a novel)*

From an Amazon Reader

"Wonderful book! I couldn't put it down. Written with a clear passion for Native American Culture and spirituality. In this story I found my own memories. It reminded me of so many teachings passed down to me. This book exceeded all my expectations. Keeping me riveted from page one; with complex characters and extraordinary care with details. I highly recommend it!"

From a Goodreads Review

"I did love this book! I have been a reader of varied subjects since a child but have always held a special affection for historical fiction of all genre. The Native history and culture of Southern Oregon is seldom touched by other authors. It was very nice to visit this world filled with insight that was written with the authority of the tribes portrayed.

"The mix of modern day and history keep the pace moving. A good suspense that made me want to know more as I turned the last page. The love story and family conflicts were realistic in their feelings. This was the first work of fiction I have ever read that explains the Great Creator of the North American Indigenous People as the same God that the Europeans brought with them."

From an Amazon Reader

"I loved this book for many reasons. The characters are well-developed. I enjoyed how each chapter was written from a different character's point of view. I thought it was a powerful story of the spiritual warfare of which we are very often unaware. I appreciated the way the author described native traditions, dress and speech . . . I look forward to reading more from this author."

Praise for *Eagle People Journal*

From Julie, an Amazon Reader

"Great food to nourish the spirit!!! A daily reading for each day of the year with a biblical reference should one choose to study further into the promises of our Creator. I can't wait for Volume II."

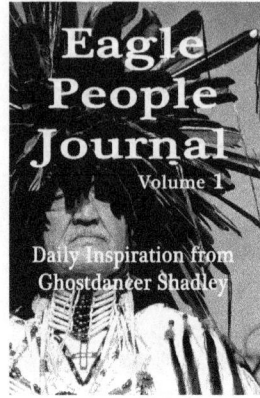

From Randy, an Amazon Reader

"This is a Christian journal/devotional that encourages, inspires and makes you think more deeply about things. And at the end of every entry, there is a scripture verse from the Bible(God's Word) to read, that seemed to have inspired the entry itself. The devotionals entry's specifically, are beautifully written and told in a Native American way. The book is also very well done, and easy to read."

From Joan, an Amazon Reader

"Ghostdancer Shadley touches your heart with daily words of inspiration on every level. Enlightenment at its best. This book is a must have for daily inspiration. A year's worth of daily reflection on a very spiritual level. The bible verse given at the end of each excerpt, gives an added lesson to be applied. Regardless of your religious background, this book is interpreted for anyone. After reading once, you will return to a special verse where the meaning becomes more powerful. A very good handbook to have for your daily inspiration."

Walking The Jesus Way

WALKING THE JESUS WAY is a term my Native American friends use for those attempting (through Spirit power) to live their lives according to the teachings of the bible (Sacred Writings) and especially according to the teachings of Jesus Yeshua.

Yeshua was not a religious man. In fact, religious people were always getting mad at him because he broke so many rules. He healed people on the Sabbath, He drank wine with his buddies, He hung out with all the wrong people, and He claimed to be the Son of God.

People who walk the Jesus Way believe in Jesus Yeshua.

To believe means to put your whole weight on this person and their teachings. That means you believe what Yeshua said enough to live according to what He says.

He says that, "God so loved the world that He gave His one and only Son that whoever believes in Him should not perish, but have everlasting life."

He also says that, "God did not send His Son into the world to condemn the world, but that the world might live through Him."

He promised that His Holy Spirit would come into our lives and remain with us if we simply believe.

He promised joy in the midst of suffering, peace during turbulent times, and hope for an amazing future. He promises to be with us at all times and forever. Nothing can separate us from His love once we place our weight on Him.

So what do you do to obtain all this?

1. You stop talking *about* Jesus Yeshua and you begin talking directly *to* Him. This is called prayer. You don't need a book to tell you how and you don't need to be in any specific position. I talk to Creator God all the time, eyes open and closed. Either way works.

2. You ask Him to forgive you for being a loser (sinner, idiot . . . whatever word you think applies best).

3. Tell Him you believe in Him and trust Him even though there's a whole lot of stuff you don't yet understand.

4. Thank Him for forgiving your sins and rising from the dead.

5. Thank Him for making you part of His family.

6. Tell someone about your decision and get with other believers on some kind of regular basis. (BTW, I would LOVE to hear from you and celebrate with you. I can be reached at sandycathcart@gmail.com)

7. Read the *Sacred Writings* (Bible). Remember to pray (talk directly to Yeshua) for guidance and direction. In doing this, you will begin to hear the Holy Spirit talking to you. The more you do this, the more you will be in tune to His voice.

When I first shared the above process with my granddaughter, she looked at me and said, "I'm not ready to make Jesus Yeshua my boss yet."

I respected Rachel's decision, because she is absolutely right . . . believing in Jesus Yeshua means you are making Him your number one Boss. She has since made that decision, and she is very glad she did! She is going for her dreams, trusting her amazing Creator every step of the way.

So are you ready to make Jesus Yeshua your boss? Are you ready to begin walking the Jesus Way?

This is a supernatural journey in a very real world. Hang onto your hat, because life is going to get exciting.

WHERE DO YOU FIT?

1. Did you just now make Jesus Yeshua your boss? If so, welcome to the family! Pray and ask the Holy Spirit to guide and teach you as you read the *Sacred Writings* (Bible). And be sure and get with others who walk The Jesus Way.

2. Have you been calling yourself a Christian but don't seem to ever get any victory in your life? Have you lost the excitement of being a child of the Most High Creator God? If so, pray and ask the Holy Spirit to renew your love for the *Sacred Writings* (Bible). Ask Him to reveal Jesus Yeshua to you in a powerful way as you read. Ask Him to help you not believe the lies of the enemy. Ask Creator God to reignite the flame in your walk with Him and give you the strength and courage to walk in a good way.

3. Did you decide that now is not the time to make Jesus Yeshua your boss? I respect that, but don't wait too long. The longer you shut out the Holy Spirit, the harder it is for you to hear His voice. Now, is a good time for you to discover who He is and what you are missing so you can make an intelligent decision. Ask God to reveal Himself to you.

"As a Lakota follower of the Jesus Way,
I endeavor to walk in the light of the Creator's presence.
I desire something akin to what the Navajo call
hozho 'the way of beauty,'
where we live in harmony with all of creation
in order to enjoy the beauty around us."
—Richard Twiss

JOY, JOY, JOY

You are the light of my darkest hours
You are the hope of my night
You are the rock that cannot be shaken
You are the strength of my life

(chorus)
And everything I've ever wanted
I've found in you and more
Everything I've ever dreamed of
Is found in you my Lord
And I find joy, joy, joy in my lowest moments
Joy in my darkest night
Joy, joy, joy that cannot be taken
Joy that will last a life

You are the friend who walks beside me
In valleys and shadows so dark
You lead the way when all is forsaken
You put the song in my heart
(chorus)

You lead the way when the path before me
Is wild and tangled and cold
You call my name and you take my hand
You promise to never let go

And everything I've ever wanted
I've found in you and more
Everything I've ever dreamed of
Is found in you my Lord
And I find joy, joy, joy in my lowest moments
Joy in my darkest night
Joy, joy, joy that cannot be taken
Joy that will last a life . . . and beyond

www.ingramcontent.com/pod-product-compliance
Lightning Source LLC
Chambersburg PA
CBHW031552040426
42452CB00006B/275